CHEATER GUIDE

Mark Fanon

Cheater Guide

How to cheat on your wife and get away with it

© Copyright 2021

Mark Fanon

www.cheater.guide

From the Man You Want to Be series

www.manyouwanttobe.com

Pearl Press

PO Box 299 Camperdown NSW 1450

Australia

ISBN 978-0-6451756-1-5

All rights reserved.

No reproduction of any part of this work is permitted in any form without prior written consent. This book is for your personal enjoyment and entertainment only. This work is published internationally and should not be construed as advice or recommendation of any action in any jurisdiction where such action breaches any law, or in any jurisdiction where such action can result in legal prejudice against you in family law or other proceedings. Any liability is excluded, including any liability for negligence, or for any loss, including indirect or consequential damages arising from or in relation to the use of this guide. Seek legal advice before proceeding.

Characters do not represent actual persons, living or dead.

A catalogue record for this book is available from the National Library of Australia

To all the men who get away with it

Contents

Who is this book for? 7
How to use this Guide 9
Legal Problems 11
Is cheating for you? 13
What's wrong with Marriage? Why Cheat? 15
The History of Cheating 18
Basic Rules 21
How to meet a new girlfriend or walk away 35
Money Money Money 46
Cover Your Tracks 51
Lift Your Game 67
Your Grooming 76
Fun Dates 82
Venues for trysts 91
Bedroom Health 95
On the Road 101
Pay to Play 103
Keeping it going 111
How to end an affair 120
How men get caught 124
When you do get caught 130
The Best Cheaters I Ever Met 133
Conclusion 139
Author Biography 141

I.

Who is this book for?

This book is about being able to have your cake and eat it too. It is about trying to stay married while enjoying all the fun you can. After reading the book, you will feel more confident that you are safe from discovery – but you must still make sure you are not too careless.

If you're a man reading this book, you will almost certainly fit into one of two types:

Reader type one— you have considered having an affair with someone and want to try it, but you think it's all too difficult. You are looking for some help to make it easier to have some fun and get away with it.

Reader type two— you are already having an affair or "getting some on the side", and you are terrified of being caught. (Perhaps you have already been caught, you promised to stop and now want to be better at covering your tracks.)

In my private Executive coaching, I have worked with recently divorced men who have spent many years out of the dating market. Unfortunately, some of these guys have completely forgotten how to appeal to, approach or keep women. This book may also help you if you fall into that category.

This book is for men, but if you're a woman brave enough to be reading it to help yourself cheat (and not a woman reading it to try and catch out your man), then you will no doubt find it has valuable ideas for you.

If you are *that* woman reading this book to catch your

husband out, think about whether you might not be happier turning a blind eye and just giving your man a break— remember, he still comes home to you, smiling.

II.

How to use this Guide

For every married man, there was a time when he was first married that it all seemed like fun. Now, years down the track, things are different. No laughs, too much hard work, endless nagging, and in many cases no sex whatsoever. Certainly never any fun, novelty, or excitement. So, it is completely understandable that you have decided to look a little further afield. Welcome to the Cheater Guide.

This book is not a simple collection of quick ideas. This is the complete guide where I explain:

How to improve your chances.
The rules to apply.
Women to avoid.
What sort of dates to take lovers on.
How to cover your tracks.
How to hide money.
How men get caught.
How to stop.
Why the very best cheaters are so successful.

As you have probably been out of the dating scene for some years, you will find the expectations of women have risen higher. So a plan is absolutely essential. From grooming to fashion, technology, online dating, health warnings, breaking up with your mistress, marriage counselling and more, this guide covers it all.

There is also a chapter devoted to Pay for Play. Many

married men avail themselves of these opportunities, but it is an area where married men need to be careful. You will also learn that there are young women who can be convinced to crossover between that world into the dating scene.

As I do in all my courses, I have placed careful consideration into the order in which this book delivers all its different lessons. I am well aware that lots of men like you reading the guide are simply going to pick the chapters and sections that sound most interesting. Feel free to do this, but rest assured, some of the biggest traps for cheaters come from the boring parts of having an affair. So, if you want to have some fun but you need to make sure you get away with it (or face minimum consequences if all goes wrong), you should read all of this guide at some point.

The lessons in this book are followed by the stories of some of my real-life experiences with different lovers. You can learn from some of these examples and discover not only what will work well for you, but also ways to avoid some of the traps for inexperienced players.

Please remember to make it as much fun as possible. (If you're not careful, you might really enjoy yourself!)

III.

Legal Problems

I am lucky enough to live in a part of the world where divorce is not based on fault. In such countries, after a separation of a year, you can simply tell a court you and your wife have irreconcilable differences, and that is that. No one needs to search for evidence of foul play. I also have the good fortune that where I live, adultery is not grounds for divorce and is most certainly not a criminal offence. If you live somewhere where adultery is a crime (The Philippines and some Middle Eastern countries, for example), either read this book and only use it when you're on vacation far away from your country or get legal advice before having an affair.

It is inconceivable to people in Europe, Australia, and New Zealand that there are parts of the world (including some US states) where home-wrecker lawsuits are still possible. These "Alienation of Affection" court cases try to sue for money as compensation for breaking up another person's marriage. If you live in one of the parts of the world where that can happen, the only approach I can suggest is to consider living somewhere else. It is also worth knowing that in some countries, such as the United States, there are special laws banning adultery for those in the military. In some parts of the world, paying sex workers is illegal. You should also know that there are parts of the world in which an unfaithful party can have worse outcomes in child custody proceedings following a divorce. So, again, get legal advice. Of course, it should go without saying that any time I use the term girls in this book, I am talking about people over the age of 18.

Ouch... now I have all that out of the way; let us quickly get to the fun parts of the book.

IV.

Is cheating for you?

"You have to accept the fact that part of the sizzle of sex comes from the danger of sex. You can be overpowered."

-Camille Paglia

Well, can you live as a cheat? If you are a married man looking to step outside your relationship for some sex, it is probably a long time since you were in the dating market. You have almost certainly forgotten the dating skills you had, and in any case— the game has changed. Nevertheless, you probably feel like your life is tedious and boring, and you're probably right. This book will teach you how to cheat and feel good, attract women, minimise complications, and part with lovers if things do not work out. I also explain what to do if you ever do get caught.

As a cheater, you're going to have to lie. At some point, you're going to be acting so much you will deserve an academy award - but if you can keep it up, you will find that you can have more fun than you have ever had in your life. If you're the sort of person who will be swamped with regrets and guilt, do not start cheating.

When I was fifteen years old, my friend Matt and I decided to go out to a dangerous but very fashionable nightclub. We both lived with our families. Our escape method we was to jump out of our bedroom windows at 2 a.m. and catch a taxi.

Neither of us had cell phones, but our plan worked. We had a great night. I later learned that Matt always left a note on his pillow for his mother when we had these adventures. He was terrified that he would make her feel bad if she could not find him for a couple of hours, and he felt guilty about it— I did not. Maybe Matt was a more considerate son than I was, perhaps he felt guilty, but he still secretly went nightclubbing underage. When it comes to cheating in your marriage, you have to decide if the guilt will be too much for you. If you are likely to do something crazy like confess without being caught, you are better off not cheating in the first place.

Some critics say that all cheaters and liars are narcissists, sociopaths and Machiavellian schemers. I think that is too harsh. Most men I know who cheat, do consider their wives. I do not pretend to be Mother Teresa, but I will point out that some of the lovers I have cheated with were not such nice people either – of course, some were simply delightful. We are all human.

his book is about cheating, real down-to-earth cheating where sex is involved. We are not talking about micro-cheating (although we will cover that later in this book), and we are not talking about open relationships. Open relationships are where everybody knows what's going on, and for some reason, everybody is happy about that. In those relationships, your wife knows that you are cheating, she might also be cheating, and you've both agreed that it's okay. If that applies to you, you do not need this book. The rest of you, those guys whose marriages have pretty much died, and who could really use some fun again, please read on. In this book, I use all of the terms: lover, side chick, mistress, girlfriend, friend-with-benefits, and sugar baby interchangeably. This is just to remind you that there are all sorts of different cheating situationships that can work for your own particular lifestyle.

V

What's wrong with Marriage? Why Cheat?

"What do I know about sex? I'm a married man."

-Tom Clancy

Nobody walks down the aisle thinking he or she is going to get divorced. It's a bit like that with staying faithful. When I got married, I firmly believed that I could remain faithful to one person (goodness knows why). In all honesty, I lasted quite a long time; well... I lasted more than a year.

Fidelity is a useful thing. For me, it's like wearing a necktie. When I'm going to an important business meeting, I wear a suit and a tie. If a guy from Mars were to land on earth, get out of his spaceship and say, "I understand most of the things you're wearing, but what's with the necktie?" I wouldn't have a sensible answer for him other than to say, "That's what most people do around here, and it works out fine".

Being married is what most people do, and it works out fine until it doesn't. One day you find that you have married the wrong person, or maybe you were too young. Perhaps as you have grown, you have changed, or she has changed? So, now you realise your marriage is not what you want it to be. You probably still love your wife, and you would rather stay married – but let's be honest for one moment – you want more. You have unmet needs around sex, intimacy and female attention. Most of all, you just need some fun.

Sometimes the problem is about you, sometimes it is about your marriage, and sometimes it is about your wife. But I am certainly not a marriage counsellor, and if you want a lesson in morality, get in touch with a priest. This book is about the other path, choosing to cheat. It is a guide for men who still like their family and their home. This is for the guys who want to stay with their kids but just want a break, an escape, a vacation without leaving home. Of course, there are risks galore, but you can make it work. I am not one of those money-hungry guys who do not want to give their ex-wife half of everything; I just do not want to get divorced.

And just in case you needed reminding, there are plenty of fun aspects of cheating:

> Your new side chick will want more sex than your wife (this will always be true, or else you just wouldn't bother spending time with her).
> Your lover will not be nagging you about budgeting, parenting, or what colour to paint the kitchen.
> A mistress will be thrilled with your company and pay you lots of attention. She will get dressed up and wear lingerie underneath.
> Your chosen girlfriend will almost certainly be younger than your wife.

You already know, just from popular culture, television, or talking to friends, that today's younger women are more interested in sex. They are more inventive in bed, and they are certainly more likely to enjoy activities that are taboo with your wife.

To put it simply, cheating is fun. While you can only have one wife, you can have more than one mistress, so you will get to enjoy variety. There will be thrills, fun, scares, highs and lows. There is no doubt that cheating will cost you money. However, if like most men reading this book, you have been married for a while and are older now, you can probably afford to spend some money on things that make you happy. Some guys spend money on golf clubs, boats, or ride-on lawn mowers. I spend money on lovers.

A twenty-five-year-old colleague at work recently suggested he might get engaged. I just chuckled, and he asked me why. I explained that he had a lot of living left in him. He then asked what I thought would be a good age for a man to get married. I replied... "maybe sixty."

VI.

The History of Cheating

"I think it is funny that we were freer about sexuality in the 4th century B.C. It is a little disconcerting."

-Angelina Jolie

Historically the concept of the other woman is well established. Whatever you call her, the mistress, the concubine, the other woman, or side chick - these have all resonated through the ages. Books and operas have been written about the greatest scoundrel lovers like Casanova. So cheating is certainly not a 21st-century phenomenon. In biblical times, multiple wives and concubines were common. King Saul and King David had plenty of wives and concubines, and King Solomon had seven hundred wives (plus three hundred concubines). Even today, if we look at our leaders around the world, we see most of the great men of the world are unfaithful.

If your marriage is far from perfect, disappoints you and leaves you wanting more, do not be too hard on yourself - marriage is not easy. Nelson Mandela was seen as a patient, kind and compassionate hero by millions, but he had three marriages. Prince Charles, the future King of England, had a mistress for many years, even though he had pretty Princess Diana waiting at home. British Prime Minister Boris Johnson has a history of affairs and children with different women.

VI | The History Of Cheating

If we look at former United States Presidents, Bill Clinton was impeached for lying about infidelity, and Donald Trump ended up paying off a bunch of porn stars. Not to mention President John F. Kennedy, whose reputation for being a womaniser has endured over fifty years.

French President Mitterrand had a love child about whose existence no one knew for decades. He clearly taught all that he knew to his young protégé Nicolas Sarkozy, who ran for President while juggling the tabloid newspaper fallout from various affairs. In the midst of it all, President Sarkozy had three wives. German Chancellor Helmut Schmidt was notorious, and Italian Prime Minister Silvio Berlusconi has been accused of all kinds of things from affairs to orgies. The former Australian Prime Minister Bob Hawke was recently described by his former mistress, later turned wife, as perpetually unfaithful.

So you're in good company. Some cultures provide for multiple wives, which would save you and me lots of problems. But, of course, nothing is as easy as it seems, so there are advantages to having a mistress with whom you can simply break up instead of yet another wife where a formal divorce is required. Unfortunately, modern Western culture bans polygamy and frowns on casual infidelity, but throughout the Muslim world, in parts of Africa and regions of Asia, polygamy is still common.

There are still many marriages where the man has fun on the side, and his wife knows, but turns a blind eye. This approach was more common some years ago. A much older friend of mine once explained to me that early on, his wife had correctly suspected that he was up to some extracurricular activities and confronted him. He was shocked when she said, "I never want to be embarrassed; it can't happen around here, I never want to find out and never want to know".

Some would say this position only exists because the woman felt that she lacked economic power and there was nothing she could do about it. I believe she is simply somebody who can deal with reality better than most. She knows her husband wants to stay with her, and she knows he wants things she does not give him. So, she decides to be practical

VII.

Basic Rules

"I'm also interested in the modern suggestion that you can have a combination of love and sex in a marriage - which no previous society has ever believed."

-Alain de Botton

There are some basic rules that you need to apply from the outset. I list them briefly here, but I shall explain them in detail during later chapters in this book. The rules are:

Keep your mouth shut!
Eyes off other women with your wife around
Lift your game.
Know who to avoid.
Practice makes perfect— You don't have to win them all.
Cover your tracks.
Always be ready to walk away.

Every time I hear about a cheating man being discovered by his wife, it turns out that he has broken one of these basic rules. In the following chapters, I explain why it is essential that you stick to *all* these rules. They are challenging but remember; if your goal is having your cake and eating it too, you must do everything necessary to maintain both sides of that equation.

Keep Your Mouth Shut!

"It's not me who can't keep a secret. It's the people I tell that can't."

-Abraham Lincoln

In *Jungle Fever*, the Spike Lee film about a black architect who cheats with his white Italian temp secretary, the hero is so happy about his new cheater life that he tells his best friend. Unfortunately, the friend, who would never knowingly betray him, just happens to have a no-secrets marriage with his own wife. When the friend shares, the wife shares, and our hero comes home to see all his clothes being thrown onto the sidewalk.

For those old enough to remember, the former American president Bill Clinton was impeached for lying about an affair. But the whole affair only came to light because the intern with whom he was sleeping decided to tell her friends. Whatever secret or deep "you and me against the world" situation you have with your lover, always assume that she is also telling her friends. For many women, relationships are about status, and they only realise that status by sharing.

Cheating is not a team sport. Do not involve your friends, your buddies at the bar or the guys at work. There are some occasions when using an ex-mistress as a wing girl can be incredibly productive, but this is only practical once you are quite an accomplished cheater.

Do not tell anyone. What good could possibly come of it? Do not brag or show off; just enjoy your affair for the pleasure that it is.

It is also important not to share too much of your private life with your mistress. Of course, the best cheaters have a

VII | Basic Rules

complete fictional persona that they can roll out at any time. The best way is to answer all of her girlfriend-style questions and dribble out small pieces of your pretend persona information, so she feels she is getting to know you. Set the expectation from the start that information will come gradually.

Why does a lover need to know the real place where you work? How many times you have been divorced? Whether or not you have kids? Decide the story that you are going to tell her and stick to it. But you have to practise enough not to mess it up, especially when you are tired, drunk, or enjoying some pillow talk after a round of steamy sex.

Let's be clear here; this book is not against micro-cheating. But if you can avoid it whenever you are with your wife, she will not be suspicious nearly so easily when she finds evidence of real cheating. Micro-cheating is the 21st-century description of flirting and similar behaviours that you really should not be doing if you are a married man. Examples commonly quoted in social media and across the Internet include:

> When you give that cute waitress a huge tip just because she smiled at you, or unbuttoned a button on her tight uniform blouse.
> Checking out hot women on social media, following your exes online or sending them birthday messages.
> Following up work meetings with good-looking women with "Nice to meet you" messages that you would never send after a meeting with a man.
> Taking off your wedding ring when you meet particular girls.
> Going out of your way to do nice things for the same girl again and again.

Some people even believe it's micro-cheating if you simply

have lunch with a woman who is not your wife or give a female colleague a ride home.

Those micro-cheating guys make that smile from a sexy woman the highlight of their boring day, but they never take the next step to become a cheater and really enjoy themselves.

Then there are the men who virtually cheat. These are the situations that get a little sexual, but you can still claim to yourself that you are not a cheater. I am talking about all of you guys who watch porn, chat with cam girls online, go to a strip club or spend time reading erotic stories.

We all know the guys who work 18 hours a day - and when they are not working, they spend the only non-work time they have, playing golf or watching football. Literally, these guys cheat their wives out of time. They are micro-cheating without even having the fun of enjoying a sexy smile.

Any time you are micro-cheating, you must make sure that your wife does not notice. The worst thing about micro cheating is that your wife will get suspicious, and you are not even doing anything especially wrong. If you plan not just to look at women but to enjoy having sex with a new lover, you have to clean up your act on all these small things because that is what it takes to avoid unnecessary suspicion at home. By all means, also pay your wife compliments, but build up to this very gradually, or she will smell a rat.

Do not look at other women when you are out with your wife— just don't. No head-turning, no comments about great fashion or nice butts. No watching music videos of hard bodied twenty-year-old singers dancing on television. No commenting at home that there's a new receptionist at work. No saying to your wife that you like her best friend's hairstyle. No matter what you think, every wife notices when you are flirting with the checkout girl or one of your adult

VII | Basic Rules

daughter's friends. Wives have a sixth sense for it. You have to gradually turn yourself into the modern version of a monk in your wife's eyes. Watch for the traps. When she says, "I think Janet has had botox", or asks you "Did you see the sexy outfit Susie was wearing?" don't pretend you didn't see, but feel free to mumble that it looked silly.

This book is about sex, not about daydreams. The way to make your extramarital sex easier and undetected by your wife, is not to micro-cheat when you are with her, ever. But, of course, when your wife is not around, the opposite is true. As discussed later in this book, you will need to practise flirting, seducing, propositioning, asking out, and starting conversations with as many women as you can, even ones with whom you do not want to sleep. If you have been married for more than a couple of years, believe me, you need the practice.

When you are not with your friends or not at work, you are pretty safe. Do not flirt or try to pick up girls when you have had a few beers and you are with your buddies. There is plenty of time to practise and succeed when you are safely alone. If you flirt with all kinds of women whenever these safe opportunities arise, your confidence and skill will improve. Soon you will be good enough to be able to have all the extra-marital fun that you want. Keep the fun in all your affairs.

"Sex is the driving force on the planet. We should embrace it, not see it as the enemy."

-Hugh Hefner

I once met Hugh Hefner in Las Vegas. We had adjoining booths at a Cabaret show. Hefner seemed completely at ease with having three gorgeous blondes with him. They were all from television shows. While of course, he did not need to spend time having a drink and a laugh with us, both Hugh Hefner and his brother could not have been friendlier to us. They were totally in their element, with lots of playmate girls falling all over them. However, the girls were just unfriendly and seemed to be having no fun. To this day, it makes me wonder, what was the point for him?

Who to avoid?

There are several entirely different approaches to cheating. This book tries to help you avoid the ones that are guaranteed to cause you problems. Things can become very complicated once you have affairs, especially if multiple women are involved. Now add into the mix that, like most of us, you probably are a busy guy anyway. To make your life easier, you need to have some ground rules. Here are the women with whom you should avoid sharing your bed.

Good fences make good neighbours

In your neighbourhood, drunken dinner parties, post-divorce cries on your shoulder, unexpected "my husband does not understand me" come-ons and more, will all provide numerous opportunities to flirt with your neighbours. Do not take things any further. Just say no to yourself and to her. You cannot change your mind later— if this woman is your neighbour, she knows your wife and where you live, and you will doubtless be seen at some point by another neighbour or family member, even if things are going well.

VII | Basic Rules

Your wife's female friends

Yes, we have all thought about sleeping with one of our wife's friends. That's right— there's that one who flirted with you that one time after a few too many drinks. Such things are entirely unsustainable. Do not do it! No matter how much fun the whole sneaky idea might be, your wife's friends should be completely off-limits. At some point they will have torn loyalties, become consumed by guilt, take therapy sessions, find religion, or hate you for something you have done at some point in the affair, and it will all backfire.

Single mothers

In that great romantic comedy *Jerry Maguire*, his footballer client criticises him for "Shoplifting the Pootie." Cuba Gooding's character explains that you must deal straight with single mothers. To my way of thinking, this is both about being decent and also about being practical. There is no doubt that a lot of fun could be had with single mothers. You will be a source of fun and enjoyment, that's a side of life she has not seen in a while, and no doubt she will be incredibly grateful. However, since single moms have little time, her opportunities will be so limited that it is unlikely she will be seeing other guys. If you date her, you effectively make her commit to you from the get-go.

Now stop and think this through from a purely practical point of view. Your time is valuable, but single mothers do not allow for any flexibility or spontaneity. They do not get away for weekends, they do not do booty calls, they cannot drop everything and come out to a restaurant because your other date flaked on you. They need to arrange babysitters and leave your date or your bed in time to be home by 10 PM or whatever their sitter agreed. In addition, single mothers must make sure they have enough money for diapers or school fees, and they will not be spending their limited cash on lingerie.

If I find out a woman is a single mom, I simply exit politely. Her world is already complicated enough.

Your staff

My forty-year-old co-worker started sleeping with one of his staff at work. She is slim, classy and ten years younger, so I can completely understand. But it did result in a divorce, drama for his kids, and of course, he needed to change jobs.

Any of you who has ever watched the TV show *Mad Men* will recall that there was a time when flirting with, or sleeping with your staff was perfectly normal and typical. However, trends in western culture have changed, and now you will find that not only does your company have rules against it, but there may also be laws about it where you live.

I'm sure you have had evenings working late when a secretary wore an outfit that showed off her breasts beautifully, or you remember the time you were at a conference and that new girl from your marketing department wore a short skirt. #MeToo. Do not sleep with her. Whether it works out well or even if it does not, one of you may have to change jobs. In addition, your work ex may well blackmail you, just to stop her from telling your wife or even your company human resources department. If you run your own business, you may have to wear an expensive lawsuit.

When viewed by other people, your happy after-work dalliance may result in you being called the next Harvey Weinstein. Sleeping with your staff or anyone junior to you at work is simply a dumb idea.

VII | Basic Rules

Avoid potentially underage girls

You might wonder why this point even needs to be mentioned, but sadly it does. A good friend of mine started a relationship with a woman he thought had finished college and was twenty-five. He was so delighted because she was not at all needy. She was happy to conduct the relationship around his schedule. It turned out she was seventeen. He found out just in time. You must be even more careful if you are talking about sugar babies or Friends with Benefits arrangements because now the girl has an added motivation to pretend to be older; money.

If you are dating younger women, you need to be super careful. Some girls love to date older guys to prove they can get an older guy or a married guy, so they could potentially be underage. If there is *any* doubt about her age, you need to see ID or just get out of there. Affairs are strictly an adults-only space.

Watch out for needy girls wanting fairy tales

Watch out for the woman who wants something more very early in the relationship. (On the other hand, if you pick up signals that the girl is after just a short-term thing or fling, then by all means, put more effort in). If it is clear that she wants something more, this doesn't rule her out, but she should move into your less desirable lovers list. The needy girl doesn't want a fun partner. She is prepared to act like one for a while as she tries to convince you that what you truly want is a life of white picket fences, with her. You open yourself up to the risk that she will go crazy when you end it— and anything could happen if she finds out you're married.

From my past: Irene the Virgin

Lesson - Who ever knows what girls are really after?

I had my profile on a sugar daddy site hidden, but it remained active, so when I was interested, I could go and take a look at available women in any city I was going to visit. One time I left my profile on, and I received the loveliest message from a woman who seemed younger than I would typically have sought out. But from what she said, we seemed to be interested in the same type of situationship.

Irene was studying in a city that I visited regularly. The next time I was in town, we had a light dinner and drinks. She seemed super keen to come back to my hotel. Suddenly she was all over me. I could not believe my luck. I did not think things like this happened to men like me. She was 20 years younger than me and, for some reason treating this older man (claiming to be divorced twice) as the perfect guy.

After I slept with her, she claimed I was her first, and we were meant to be, and we should get married. I tried to slow things right down. I did see her a few more times before I had to explain to her that although I enjoyed her company (in and out of bed), I was never going to be her knight in shining armour. She took it very well. About three months later, she sent me an invitation to her wedding. I declined, thinking to myself, "poor guy".

Do not accept Damaged Goods!

One of the worst things that can happen is that you may get involved with a crazy, clingy woman. Many years ago, there was a movie called *Fatal Attraction*. In this movie, a woman was rejected after having a weekend affair with the

VII | Basic Rules

married star of the film whilst his wife was away. The woman, played beautifully by Glenn Close, turns absolutely crazy when Michael Douglas' character does not want to continue the affair. She torments him at work, she stalks him at home, and she even kills his children's pet in the infamous bunny boiler scene.

I have heard even crazier things. One guy I know claims he broke up with a girl when she turned up with his name tattooed on her hip. They had been together only four weeks! Watch out for any woman who: won't take no for an answer, keeps calling or texting you, turns up unannounced, or seems to have a split personality. I feel bad that I once broke up with a girl after taking a sneak peek in her medicine cabinet and realising that she had lots of medications for a chemical brain imbalance.

Secrecy is the only way to avoid the problems that could come from a bunny boiler. If she has limited details of yours, you can get out of there alive.

From my past: Megan the Checkout Girl

Lesson - Crazy girls exist.

I met Megan on one of those seeking sites where you arrange to meet sugar babies. She lived in a city that I visited every two weeks for business and, from our brief online and text banter, it seemed like she would be low-maintenance fun—just the perfect girl for what I had in mind.

During a fun dinner, Megan explained that she worked on a supermarket checkout aisle. All she was looking for was a friend with benefits who could take her out to classy restaurants whenever he was in town. Of course, she was happy to spend the night with him afterwards. Following a few glasses of wine, Megan suggested that we go to a cocktail bar. I had not expected to sleep with her on our first date, but she was so open towards me that I suggested we try the cocktail bar at my hotel. She was instantly positive about the idea.

Immediately upon arrival, she ordered tequila shots. I enjoy a cocktail, but tequila is not one of my poisons. Nevertheless, I had two tequilas. Megan had six or seven shots in succession. That is, until all hell broke loose. First, this girl started throwing glasses around the bar. Soon she started throwing furniture; next Megan was taking off her clothes.

Security came to me and asked if I wanted them to handle her or whether they should call an ambulance. I stayed in this hotel every two weeks, so I was deeply embarrassed. I grabbed her and took her away from the bar and to my hotel room. After throwing whatever she could find at me, Megan eventually sat in the corner of the room for about six hours while she sobered up. Finally, I put her in a cab and sent her home in the pre-dawn light.

I was feeling understandably worse for wear and tired in one of my business meetings that morning when I received the following text:

> Dinner last night with you was just amazing. I am ever so sorry about what happened. The good news is that you have seen me at my worst, and I assure you it will never happen again. I know I have alcohol-induced psychosis. But I do not want it to spoil what might be my only opportunity to ever get to know a man like you. If you are willing to see me again, I promise I will make it up to you in ways you can dream about.

I pressed *delete*.

VII | Basic Rules

From my Past: Louise the publicist

Lesson - *Avoid damaged goods.*

Louise was a long-term friend of mine, one of the few side chicks who knew my true identity and had also met my wife. I was vaguely aware Louise had previously experienced some mental health issues, but that was years ago, and I was happy she was doing well and back to her old self. We regularly caught up for lunch just as friends. One day Louise explained she was in a real financial bind. I loaned her $900, and she said she would return it in a couple of weeks. As with all loans to friends and family, in my mind, I was prepared for the money just to be a gift. Imagine my surprise when she called my office three weeks later and suggested I drop by her place because she had my money for me. When I arrived the following lunchtime, she handed me an envelope and said, "Here is your $500". I do not know what one should do when somebody returns you an amount of money different to the sum they borrowed, but I was amazed I got back any of it. I should have guessed that all was not okay with her.

A few weeks later, after a five-hour-long alcohol-fuelled Italian lunch, we went back to her place and started making out (we hadn't for years). Things very quickly became steamy and sexy and soon were both half-naked. It seemed like after being friends for so many years, we were finally going to do the deed. Suddenly, Louise leaped up and raced out of her apartment screaming, "There's a crazy man in my apartment, I think he's a rapist". She was getting louder and louder, so I chased after her, half-dressed. Whilst I was trying to calm her down, two huge neighbours who looked like they lived for the gym and took too many steroids came racing towards me. I took off down the fire stairs and have never seen her since.

Decide if married women are even worth it

Lots of people will tell you that you should have your extramarital affairs with married women. The false reasons these so-called experts will give you include:

Married women will have the same stake in keeping the affair secret that you have.

Married women will not suddenly want to take over your life and get rid of your wife because they have a life at home.

I try to avoid married girls. There are lots of risks. Because you are both in the same situation, you are far more likely to let slip some of the details of your life outside the affair.

It is not uncommon for married women to be using the affair as a revenge tactic to get even on their own cheating husband. They will possibly use you as a trophy to show him they can cheat too. You will then have a cuckolded husband to deal with, as well as a talkative lover.

Because a married woman's situation is so complicated, you will often have no say in when your affair ends. This is downright annoying, especially if one of the reasons you like extramarital romances is because you can be in control of when they start, and you can end them.

With a married lover, you will always remain her plan B. She is probably still sleeping with her husband, and she is certainly not giving all her attention, love, and all those things which make you feel special, only to you.

You will discover that the married woman will not be flexible with her timing. Her lack of availability for getaways and dates means she may not be able to fit in with your cheater schedule. As a result, your fun, relaxed affair may soon seem like endless rushing and complex diary management.

VIII.

How to meet a new girlfriend or walk away

You are all grown up now, so you know that you cannot just guess your way through every situation. Since sleeping with women other than your wife can be tricky, the best thing is to make a plan and work through it.

Train your wife

Part of your planning to enjoy dates and great sex with multiple women is training your wife. You should start now before the affair, because over time, you have to get your wife to become accustomed to a whole lot of changes that make it easier for you to cheat. These include: that you sometimes work late, that you travel for business, that you cannot always answer your phone, and that you do not have much holiday leave built up at work. It is best to start this when you are relatively innocent, and she can check up on you and discover that it is only normal or business as usual for you. Of course, later you will want all these opportunities to cover up your affairs.

Many pundits say if a guy who has been married for a long time starts taking care of his appearance, his wife should be worried about an affair. The correct way to manage this is to get her involved like it is her idea. For example, if your wife mentions that you are putting on weight, respond that "Yes, I had better get to the gym". You should start exercising now or, at the very least, taking time out for runs or long walks. I will explain later why that is a great idea. If your wife ever comments on any of your old clothes, agree with her. Talk about how you need a wardrobe update. It is always useful to say you are being considered for a different job or a management role at work as a reason to take care of your appearance or start to dye your hair.

You should have a rationale for why you are into any new hobbies you have learned from your lovers, like wine tasting or French movies. Plan it all now so that you can start dropping hints and also so you will have great answers when the questions come.

Ring Ring

What to do about a wedding ring is always a difficult question. The obvious answer, of course, is do not wear one in the first place. I have been that guy who is always taking it on and off. It is more trouble than it is worth. While undressing, I once dropped my "hidden" wedding ring from my suit pocket right in front of a gorgeous friend with benefits who thought I was single. I had not seen her for ages, and I simply explained that I had remarried.

You do not want to give your wife any suspicion that you are cheating, but you also must avoid being the guy with the faint line around your finger when you are on a date. One of the best approaches is to have a good excuse not to wear a wedding ring. Try these:

Safety on your job (mechanics often do this).

Claiming that you have simply lost the ring will last you for a while, but you may have to get another ring— this will cost you money, and you will be back where you started.

The best excuse of all is that the ring no longer fits you.

VIII | How To Meet A New Girlfriend Or Walk Away

This gives you plenty of time, while you can claim you need to lose weight (or put on weight, whichever sounds more likely). This is easier than paying to have it adjusted.

Finding your girlfriends

One thing that you should remember, to give yourself some confidence, is that since you are a married man, at some time, you managed to convince a woman not only to go out with you but to marry you. You also clearly had what it takes to get her into your bed. So, you are starting at a point where I assume you already know the basics of how to pick up girls, and things to do on dates.

I teach classes to some men whose lives sound quite impressive, but they are completely hopeless in this area. Some of those guys go to pieces when trying to ask a woman for a date or get her into bed. Since you are married and improving by reading this book, your skills already will put you far ahead of all those other guys. But, believe me; even those guys can be coached, so you just need a refresher and a little polish. That is what we cover in the rest of this chapter.

Let's start with the traditional way - approaching and choosing girls in person

Okay, since you are completely out of practice, you must remember to flirt. Only do this *when your wife is not around!* You start by talking to people, smiling, being friendly and making small jokes. Ask questions of any woman you meet. She can be the girl in line at the supermarket, the barista who makes your coffee, or the waitress at your lunch café. The idea here is to get yourself so relaxed that you will be approachable, smiling and accustomed to talking to girls. You mustn't wait to practise just on the pretty woman, or that perfect available single woman you want to sleep with. You have to get used to smiling and flirting with every woman.

When you are starting, ideas you need to keep in your head are:

Whatever ends up happening with this one doesn't matter. She can be a trial for the one you want.

Even if this woman seems perfect, you still have a wife you can go home to, so you do not need anyone in particular to be your next lover.

Who cares if she says, "Go away"?

Won't it be great if she is really into me?

After you have been rehearsing flirting, smiles and friendliness for a while (without your wife around), the time comes to ask a woman for her phone number, and at some point, for a date. Do not beat around the bush, it is far better just to state what you have in mind, or to ask her directly. You will save a lot of time, and at least you will know if she is interested. You will not, as the Australians say, die wondering. It is okay to test her or challenge her, you are deciding if she could work for you, and there is always another girl.

Banter to and fro is okay. There is a fine line between testing her and being creepy, but guys reading this book probably know this already. When you are practising you will hear lots of responses like "I have a boyfriend", "I think I am busy all next week" or "I do not date people I meet at work". Girls commonly say things like this. Sometimes they are true, and sometimes they are merely tests. Either way, the better you get at meeting women, the fewer negative responses you will encounter and the less you will be concerned about rejection. Like the old salesmen say, every woman you meet takes you closer to meeting the right one.

In the movie *Falling in Love*, Robert De Niro's character

asks Meryl Streep's character if she would like to join him for some lunch. Her immediate response is that she's married. De Niro's character simply says, "Married people have to eat too!" She joins him and what follows is a special relationship between two married people.

Talk to Women every day

You can ask a girl about the book she is holding in the store; you can check if she knows what time the next train is, you can ask what food is good at this café. You can say, "What an interesting pin on your sweater!" or "Wow, those shoes look great, but how do you dance in them?"

Once you feel quite at ease approaching women and talking with them, you can spend more of your time focusing on which girls to approach to get the most bang for your buck. A lot of this will come down to assessing body language. Notice what you are doing with your body (open, friendly, approachable) and think about what she is doing with her body.

How is she sitting or standing? Does she want someone to talk to her? Look at her upper body and shoulders if she has already seen you. Has she turned towards you? If she is smiling at you warmly, is her stance open, so she is not blocking you off? Are there things placed in front of her body like a handbag or purse - or are they moved to the side, indicating a welcoming manner? Does she flick her hair? (I believe that women cannot help making this sign, and it is rarely planned.) Does she touch her lips with her tongue or fix her lipstick after she has seen you? All these postures and gestures are highly welcoming signs. Once you believe you would be welcome, look at her eyes – just a little longer than you think feels comfortable for you. Then look away. Look back; if your gaze returns to see a smile, go talk to her.

Once you are well-practised flirting with and talking to women who do not necessarily matter to you, your nervousness and your fear of rejection will both have worn off.

Now remember all the things a woman is looking for from any man who asks her out:

A confident guy.

Someone who might be fun.

A man who seems trustworthy.

Give off these vibes, and you will meet with success. Just make sure nothing you do comes across as needy or creepy.

So things are moving along nicely; now you have a woman who has seemed responsive to your initial interest in her. She has shown some interest in you. You have decided that she is not too local (it is never a good idea to have lovers who live in your neighbourhood or shop at the same shopping mall.) So how are you going to ask her out? Sometimes you can ask her face to face, and sometimes you need to get her number and follow up later. It is a good idea just to *suggest* she give her number to you. For example, "Here, give me your number. I would love to have a Japanese dinner with you on Thursday." As well as getting the number and portraying confidence, it also means that you are already steering away from your conversations being carried out on her social media. For you, social media has all sorts of privacy problems.

Once you have her number, you can text or call. Younger women may be surprised by a call, but it can still work, and they may enjoy the difference. For older women, either is fine.

Textiquette

Think carefully about your texting game as the relationship progresses. You may think you know how to text, but your texting game is twenty years out of date, and to her, your

VIII | How To Meet A New Girlfriend Or Walk Away

texts will be like watching a twenty-year-old football game on TV is to you. Players seem to be trying hard, but it is not what you are used to in the modern game.

Always try to make your texts light and flirty. Funny is always good. The best texts leave her wondering about something, so she has to ask you more. Good flirty texts often include a question, this way you are likely to get a reply. When she texts you, do not reply immediately. Just don't. It is okay to leave as much time between your texts to her as she leaves between her texts to you (and even longer is better).

There is nothing wrong with asking her to text you when she gets home from a date to make sure she gets home safe. If you did not do that, and if she has not messaged you a day or so after a date, you can text her something funny that indicates you enjoyed it. Likewise, there is never a problem with you texting her the morning after you first sleep with her, she will appreciate the reassurance, and you are setting yourself up for a fun second time.

I can't stop thinking about...

Is a text you can send that almost always gets a reply. Think of a safe and fun follow up for when she asks:

About what?

You should never be sexting or sending highly suggestive sexual texts until you have slept with a woman twice. Remember, no matter how much you like looking at them— always delete her texts. If they are romantic or sexy, delete them right away so you cannot forget or change your mind. You must not have that kind of evidence anywhere.

From my Past: Sakura, the geologist

Lesson - Social Proof you are a confident man always works

I was at a huge international conference in Europe with a group of men in what was a very male-dominated industry. One of the few women at the end-of-day cocktails function in a room of 200 was a gorgeous Japanese girl. She was surprisingly tall, slim, and dressed as if she had just stepped off the catwalk. She was standing by herself just away from the bar. I was married but away from home, feeling relaxed, brave, and I had nothing to lose. I was not looking for an extramarital fling and had never dated an Asian girl. I strolled over to the beautiful Japanese woman standing alone and asked her to join our group (of three guys). While we were introducing ourselves, one of the guys, my counterpart from our New York office asked Sakura where she was from. She simply answered, "Japan." He pressed on and asked her whereabouts in Japan, although he had never been there.

"Hiroshima."

My colleague would not let it drop. "Didn't we really bomb your guys good in World War II?" Then, just when I thought the sky was going to open up and swallow us all, the gorgeous Sakura simply smiled and stated, "I am going to the bar to grab another cocktail and will be back in a moment". As soon as she moved away, World War three broke out between my international colleagues. "Are you crazy? How could you say that?"

"Well, we did bomb them, and they deserved it!"

As the most senior guy from our company, I explained to my colleagues in no uncertain terms, that this was not how we were going to conduct ourselves. Although I was sure that Sakura had not understood what had been said because her

VIII | How To Meet A New Girlfriend Or Walk Away

face had not changed for a second from its lovely smile, I still felt some guilt. So, I walked over to the bar to try and organise my own private peace conference. I started by telling her how lovely it was to have some women at the conference and how happy I was to have met her. She explained that she was completely used to all men in our particular industry. A drink or two later, I mentioned that it was a great thing that she had not caught some of the remarks of my colleagues as they could be very rude.

"What do you mean I did not hear their comments? I am Japanese, not deaf".

But it was quite clear that she had understood that I had defended her honour and that I was a guy who had no problem putting the others in their place. I think it was this proof of social status that worked with Sakura, and she and I drank the night away. We ended up sharing a room for the next four nights.

Sakura was just a lucky opportunity. In those days I didn't plan to cheat and so I was not well-prepared. Although I was clever enough to let her believe I was divorced, I made the mistake of only using one phone, and so Sakura had my main cell phone number. Five long years after we had broken up, I received a birthday text message which was quite romantic, reminding me of something we had done on my birthday six years prior. It was pure luck that my wife did not see it as she picked up my phone and simply passed it to me.

Finding girls online is tricky

Regular dating sites intended for single people pose problems for a married man. As you would expect, the problem is around secrecy. You do not wish to have your wife, her friends or family seeing you on a dating site or being told that you are there. That is simply more trouble than it is worth.

The only time I think it makes sense to use a regular dating site or an app like Tinder is if you are travelling to a different country or a city nowhere near anyone you know. Traditional dating sites do not work without photos, and you certainly do not want yours to be displayed. Remember to delete any dating apps from your phone when you come home. Later, in the chapter on *Pay to Play*, I discuss arrangement sites and how these differ from standard dating sites in the online world.

Online dating

Many guys who cheat make their lives difficult by using regular dating sites. The main problem with traditional dating sites is that most of them need your photo displayed, and if it is not your wife who sees your picture there, it will be her sister or your babysitter.

These sites should only be used when you are a long way from home, in a different city or even out of your country. The same applies to apps like Tinder. If you are going to be away for several days, you may wish to use these apps to arrange dates, but the best ones will be the ones that arrange dates based on exactly where you are right now, like Tinder or like features in WeChat. There is no point using a dating site when you are away from home if it allows your wife to enter locations and look at matches in other cities as well. Sometimes the web version of a dating app will let you enter a location to check, whereas the app version will automatically use phone location-based services.

Make sure you delete the app before you get home; you do not wish your wife to find the app on your phone. It is also critically important that you do not use any photo of yourself on these apps that has ever been used anywhere else for anything. It is super simple these days for someone to use either Google image search or TinEye reverse photo searches and find your dating photo matches up with a family photo, social media photo or work photo of you.

There are some specialised apps for only married people to hook up, I have not experimented with these, but I have concerns about their privacy. All the women on them know you are married, which never suits me; any hackers looking for targets will also know you're married. I steer clear.

If you do not mind friends-with-benefits situationships, there are specialised *arrangement* websites, and I write about these elsewhere in this book. However, if you are going to use regular dating apps despite it being risky, check the section in this book on Pay to Play and follow my advice there on how to develop sugar daddy profiles.

Walking away

Don't feel you have to stay the course with the wrong woman. There is little chance that the girl you have just met is truly Ms Wonderful. It is far more likely that she is putting on an excellent front for a first date. Just because she said yes to you for a date does not mean you need to continue to see her if you are not interested.

Whenever you are looking for a lover, make it so that you can always walk away – or she can. Be prepared to move on and exit gracefully. Remember, you still have your marriage, and you can always have another affair.

IX.

Money Money Money

In almost every case, if you are going to be conducting extramarital affairs, you will need some money. This applies even if she is not a kept mistress or you're not technically paying for play, (which is a polite name for paying escorts or sugar babies, more of that later). There are other books in the Man You Want to Be series that teach ways to get yourself to financial freedom, and you may find they help you afford a lot more fun in the longer term.

There are two sides of the money problem that you have to remember: One is you need the money to spend on your new dates, the second is that you need to make sure that you do not leave your wife any traces of places you were not supposed to be on receipts, credit card bills or bank statements.

So how do you keep money from your wife? There are four traditional ways:

> Method 1: Having some of your pay, salary or wages going to a different bank account.

It is hard to set this up when you are used to having a certain amount of money coming into your regular account, especially if you have joint bank accounts with your wife. The time to do this is around the time of the year when salary increases happen, or whenever you change jobs. Then, you just go to your pay office and tell them to have the salary increase put into a different account, your new online-only account.

At one point in my career, I was running a large business and had several hundred staff. One day, at a company Christmas Party, a woman I had never met approached me with fire in her eyes and said I was a horrible boss. She said her husband was a decent man who worked hard, and yet I had not given him a pay rise in five years. (Her husband was a great employee, worked hard and as a result, had got pay rises every single year). Of course, I kept his secret safe, but internally I smiled and hoped he was spending his hard-earned money in ways that made him happy.

Method 2: Hoard the money any time you get a bonus:

Anytime you're getting a bonus of any sort or a big commission payment (or some unusual amount your wife cannot be certain that you will receive), ask the pay office where you work, to put that money into your other account.

Methods one and two could cause a problem if your wife is financially literate and does your tax returns or goes through your pay slips— just remember that.

Method 3: Cash spending that sounds believable:

You need to find something that your wife knows nothing about (or shows no interest in) and then find a way you can say you had to pay for it in cash. For example, many guys say they have a mechanic friend, and if they pay him in cash, he will service their car cheaply. You could explain about a buddy who will give you new tyres for half price, but only if pay him in cash. Of course, the work never really happens, but as your wife does not know or care about wheels or your automotive repairs, suddenly you have some cash in your pocket to spend. You can withdraw money from your savings and checking account in many countries by simply asking for some cash out when you are shopping in a supermarket with your debit card. This way, you can buy $100 of groceries, but end up with cash in your pocket plus a supermarket charge on your account, which says $200. This works well to build up a cash stash over time. Buying gift cards at supermarkets or department stores to inflate your shopping bill is also effective; just remember to throw out the underlying receipts every time.

Method 4: The work expenses recycle:

Are you in the sort of job where you use your private credit card or spend your own money on things for work, and your company reimburses you or pays back your expenses? This is the perfect opportunity to have your company finance department pay those into your separate, fun bank account. Gradually, money comes out of your regular salary to pay for company expenses but ends up funding your extra-curricular side activities.

Your fun bank account

Do you have an old account from before you were married? Do you have a side account, one that was for another purpose like investments or left over from college days? This could be your fun account. This account should be only in your name, so it does not pop up when your wife opens a banking app and sees shared accounts. Even accounts which claim to be entirely online will occasionally send bank letters or other paperwork to you. This is usually when they're trying to offer you an upgrade, when they couldn't get in touch with you (for example, your email was temporarily down) or, in the case of an overdraft or a credit card, if you forget to pay a bill. So much for your "online-only" account. The trick here is to use your office address as the postal address. Having done that, you will probably never get a letter, but if you do will be easier to apologise to someone at work for a silly letter than it will be to have your wife open it and ask why you use that bank or what account this is all about. Be especially careful any time you change addresses because some banks will send you a letter to the old address to confirm the change.

Remember that credit applications, especially with a new bank - can be flagged in a credit report that our wife may one day see. This is not a show-stopper, but it is worth having your excuse planned well ahead of time.

Never forget that for a cheater, cash is king. (Yes, even in these contactless post-COVID days). However, for many restaurant bookings and for checking into hotels, you are still going to need to use a credit or debit card. (Often, you can settle in cash at the end, even if you checked in with a card.)

Frequent Traveller Points

My favourite way to fund things is not to use dollars at all and just use points. There are two schools of thought on this because of the records that are created, but for me, this is where frequent flyer miles, hotel points, or any sort of frequent traveller scheme really comes in handy. It lets you have fun while minimising your chances of being caught dipping your hand into the marital bank account. Even if you do not fly or stay in hotels for work, you may already have (or be able to switch to) a credit card that gives you points for spend on basic regular things. Take the points!

You can then use these points to pay for flights, hotels and in some cases restaurants and other things. Add to that that the points game can simply be fun. There is no shortage of guides, forums and podcasts on the Internet to get you up to speed, especially if you travel for work. Just make sure you turn off any paper statement options, so your wife will never know how you are accumulating or spending points. The thing that I enjoy most is using my points for business class upgrades for my lovers and me on planes and to get suite upgrades at hotels. Also, if you reach a certain status with most of these programs, you get access to lounges and clubs. All these things can be very appealing to a young woman happy to be with a man of the world.

X.

Cover Your Tracks

Cover your digital tracks

It is the 2020s, and no matter how you meet your new girlfriend, it is highly likely that you will be doing most of your communication with her electronically. You will use your phone, your computer, or other devices to keep in touch with her and arrange meetings. While this is convenient, the problem is that all digital devices leave tracks.

When you get lazy (and we all do), or when your wife decides she is suspicious and wants to spy, there will be evidence galore. This chapter gives you enough information to cover your tracks. Still, you should keep up-to-date in this area, as technology moves very quickly and what is sufficient privacy and security today may not be enough quite soon. You will probably think that this chapter is over-complicating things. I am simply trying to give you a complete picture. I know that like most guys, you will not follow many of these tips. Security is a habit, not a switch you flick or a purchase you make. The more you practise, the better.

I have already recommended using a different name to conduct your cheating, perhaps your middle name, and different occupation or company. The best way to make all this work is to create a new online identity. At its simplest, having a new identity means you set up a new name or nickname, a new phone number, a new email account for your new name, and make sure your wife cannot access any of them. It is easy and free to set up a new email account on a regular service such as Gmail or for more security, you could even use protonmail. Make sure you use a different mail client program for your new email account. There is no point having the cheater account set up as another mail account on your outlook. You don't want autocomplete showing embarrassing past email addresses or lover emails popping up at the wrong moment. I only access this account from a webmail browser and clean out all my web cache every session. You should also make sure you do not have unnecessary features like copying all mail to yourself switched on. Unless there is a special need to keep old emails or attachments like pictures that can incriminate you, just delete them all.

Use two-factor authentication. These days most email providers and social media platforms will allow you to have a secondary form of confirmation each and every time you try and log in. For example, when you try and sign into a Google or Gmail account on a computer, your account can be set up to require you to accept on your phone that somebody is logging in. Most banks already do this and anywhere you can, I strongly recommend you do this for your private accounts. Your suspicious wife will quite simply not be able to log in without access to your phone. Even better, you will discover that she was trying.

Phones

The main way you will get in touch with your lovers is by using the phone. But if you have reached this point in this book, you will realise that it is a bad idea to have your new girlfriend contacting you on the same number as your wife. You want to be able to have one woman on silent - or going to voice mail - and the other able to reach you, depending on which woman you are sitting next to right then. Some married men who enjoy cheating with a girlfriend or mistress, like to set up customised ringtones for their family. They can then decide whether or not they wish to answer a phone call, depending on where they are or who might be around to overhear, without having to stop and suspiciously check the phone screen.

Ideally, you want a second phone with a different phone number. How you explain this to your wife is the tricky part. Most men usually claim to have a work phone and personal phone. The work phone can use a prepaid SIM so that it does not appear on your phone bill (if your wife sees those). If you wish to tell your lovers that you live in a different place, you can also get a SIM from there, and you will be able to present a different area code when you call.

Although it is best, having a different phone has some cost (although you can use a cheap phone and a prepaid SIM, which does not cost much for limited use), and it can raise suspicion with your wife. If you do need to use a single phone you can follow the example of some men who have a second SIM card. They can then put that card in and out when they want to call or text messages from the girlfriend. If you have a messaging app as your main contact, you can message her using either.

Did you ever wonder why you see all these guys out walking their wife's or children's dog in the evening? These guys were using the opportunity to go out and make a phone call to their mistress or swap to a different SIM.

Some people simply use Google phone to divert calls from a different number to their phone. This is only available however in a limited number of countries (and at this stage seems to be only in North America). There are other services such as Hushed, which combine messaging apps and giving you a new phone number that can be dialled from a regular phone. These have some charges attached for usage.

Dual-SIM phones are fashionable in some parts of the world. They are typically used by people who travel to several countries. The older ones have two physical SIM slots in the phone. The newer phones have an eSIM which is simply downloaded from your network carrier, as well as a standard physical SIM. Check with your phone company.

While it is possible to manage two numbers on one phone, I find this is not as good as having separate phones because there are many times when you simply want to put one phone away or switch it off and not think about it. You also want to make sure you do not make mistakes when using the other phone number, (not surprisingly, these things always seem to happen after you have had a few drinks or when you are exhausted). Many men have been caught out sending messages from the wrong number, or having their wife see things that should never have been on the main phone. It is a lot easier to keep track of and secure everything about your affairs on your cheater device.

If you have a second phone number, memorise it. Sometimes you have to say it out loud with your girlfriend there, like giving that number for a restaurant booking or putting it on anything your lover might check, like an air ticket. It gets silly when you are not able to put your own phone number into a girl's phone... all because you do not even know it. If the relationship continues to develop the way you hope, you will be messaging her, and she will be able to enjoy seeing your name come up.

Your phone should be password protected. It can then be

turned on by face, fingerprint or pass code. You can even get apps that put passwords in front of individual applications on the phone even when you have unlocked the phone. A suspicious wife will always find a reason to ask for your phone PIN at some point. If you refuse, that is highly suspicious. The only solution is always to keep your phone exceptionally *clean*, so your wife can do whatever trivial thing she claims to need it for, without seeing anything incriminating. If this happens and you did give her your password, keep your phone clean afterwards, but do not change your password or PIN to something else immediately. It makes you seem too suspicious. The best idea is to wait a while, e.g., two or three weeks and then change it. If later your wife does ever query why you changed it again, explain you change all your passwords every month or two.

Make sure you set your phone to lock itself automatically quite quickly after being used. This can be set to just seconds instead of several minutes. You can also set up your smartphone so that you choose whether to see notifications for messages on the screen when the phone is locked. My preferred approach is to have a notification that there is a message, but never display sender or a preview of any messages unless I am using the phone and choose to open up messages. Phones keep logs and it is vital to edit or delete all messages, logs and phone calls sent to and from your lover on your phone. This is true, whichever phone you are using. Because you cannot always delete things immediately when they happen, you should be checking your phone regularly for undeleted messages which you simply forgot to clean up.

It is important that you and your wife do not share the same Apple iCloud or Google accounts to set up your phones. Although this is quite common with married couples, just a few clicks changing the settings will let your wife see all your calls and messages as they happen. Get your own accounts. Be extra careful if the same account is used on a television or kitchen display. Some people have their phones set up to also send their text messages to their computers, or even display them on a tablet, an iPad or a car display. Do not do this! Imagine what will happen when your wife is looking over your shoulder at a shopping catalogue or watching a funny kitten video and suddenly up pops a message thanking you for the great time you showed your girlfriend in bed last night.

Do not be too clever, it is not uncommon for a careful cheat to have the details of his lover or side-chick in only one device, (this could be on your phone stored as another name like a colleague). If you lose the phone and are not technically savvy enough to be able to restore a remote back up, you might never be able to get in touch with her again. After all the work you have put in, that would be tragic. Always have a second method of getting in touch with her or an alternative place where you have recorded her details, safely under a different name.

Tracking

A modern smartphone tracks you. The only way it will ever stop tracking you is if you turn the power completely off. What your phone does with its tracking information is what matters to you. There are settings in Apple and in Google Android and other systems which will control whether your phone or tablet *keeps* your location data. By default, some devices keep track of every place you ever were, and a week or a month later, you can bring up a map and see everywhere you have been. I do not need to explain why this is a bad idea for a cheater.

The only way to get around this is to turn off location

services. All phones have privacy settings that allow you to do this. You can turn off the location services for the whole phone (this is a problem when you want to use things like navigation), or you can turn off location services, app by app. I prefer to turn off location services entirely and only turn them back on when I need them. You can also go into privacy settings on your Google or Apple accounts and modify how long history is kept (if at all).

Think of what traps your wife could lay for you if she does get a hold of your phone for a few minutes. Imagine the shock one man found when he realised his wife had used the Uber settings in his phone to make herself a trusted contact so that she can have access to his travel movements. Likewise, if you have *find my phone* services activated, someone with access to your password will know where you have been.

I believe it is also worthwhile turning off locations for the camera app on your phones. This works two ways; you do not want a lover to find details of where you live with your family, and you do not want your wife to find details of where you have been with your lover. These details can often be discovered from a photograph, especially if uploaded onto the net or some shared resource. You can remove geocoded data and EXIF data from photos, but why allow location on there in the first place?

Other problem phone apps?

Some women put apps on the phones of their whole family so they can see where their entire family is at any time. This is usually set up to keep track of the children, but it can also keep track of her husband. Many modern apps such as Snapchat have a feature that shows where friends are. Anytime you can see where other people are, they can probably see where you are if you have the wrong settings. Location services need to be turned off.

All navigation apps such as mapping apps and even your car nav system can keep track of where you are, make sure you do not enter problem addresses without remembering to delete or clear them. Recently, there a host of new apps such as COVID venue check-in apps and exposure notifications which can keep track of where you are, and if you are not careful, could display details to your wife next time. Careful -by peering at your phone over your shoulder, she could learn your last check-in location while you are doing something as innocent as entering a restaurant with her.

Schedule a regular privacy sweep day in your diary to check and clean everything in this chapter.

Choosing a Messaging app

It will be easiest to keep track of your communications and keep them secure if you always use the same messaging channel. As a result, many people like to use messaging apps as an alternative to SMS text messaging. Among the more common smartphone messaging apps that you may find easier or safer are:

WhatsApp— it links to an actual phone number but is used worldwide. She is probably already on this.

Kik— this anonymous one is popular with the sugar baby or FWB set.

Skype— you can easily create a free account using Hotmail or Outlook email.

Line—anonymous app, popular in ASEAN countries across Southeast Asia.

WeChat— a China-based social media service. I use it in Asia, where it is a default that seems to replace Facebook and Twitter. Not only is it great for communication separately to channels your wife will ever use, but it has a feature which can be used for a *who is nearby?* type of hook-up.

There are others with different features. Although they are less common, Viber, Signal, and Telegram all have auto-destruct features that can make messages disappear after an amount of time. If you are ever going to use a photo, profile, or even an avatar on any messaging app, remember that it should not be a pic that you have ever used anywhere else, and never use it again.

Social media

Don't even think about adding your new girlfriend or mistress to your current social media account friends list. If you use real name social media apps in your personal life, as well as not connecting your new lover as a friend, make sure that you turn on privacy and perhaps use something rather than a picture of yourself as your profile picture. You do not want a girlfriend or a former lover that you were happy to have forgotten and dismissed to your past, to find you again randomly.

If you really need to have a cheater social account (and this usually only applies to the younger married guys), you can create a whole new set of social accounts based on your new email. But why bother? It is more discreet not to have them at all. If you go ahead and insist upon using a cheater social media account with your new identity, start by blocking anyone who you wouldn't want to be able to see your cheater account if they snooped, like your friends, family (and your wife).

A former colleague explained to me recently that he had been having great success meeting women on Clubhouse. This app is relatively new, and it is hard to know how popular it will be long-term. It suits some men who feel happier in an audio chat based upon large group chats with breakout rooms. However, I am concerned about some of the privacy aspects, and I feel it may be better for the single guys.

PC safety and Internet security

Your PC is a great way to keep in touch with women, use dating apps or seeking apps, make reservations, and store notes. But anyone with access to your computer will have access to a treasure trove of evidence. Always have a password on your computer. Always have security systems and anti-virus systems running and up-to-date.

Having what are known as strong passwords is essential; many people find it easiest to use a password manager. Two of the more common ones are NordPass or LastPass. You should be very careful if you use Google Chrome browser passwords or similar to store passwords for dating or escort sites. Suppose your wife has access to your computer or chrome password. She may well be able to see which websites you keep stored passwords for, even if she cannot access the individual accounts, and that could cause you problems.

As a married man, you often need to worry about what women say about you after your breakup. If your lover discovers that you were married and she did not know, and she has your full life details, she could be the worst type of enemy. Often her revenge comes by writing nasty things about you online on the Internet. There are even some websites devoted explicitly to shaming men. Therefore, it is vital that you check what is written about you under your real name and any of your fake names. You should also check comments about your phone numbers on the internet. A tip is to enter your phone number in multiple formats as a search term just to make sure you catch everything. Once again, I make a diary note for the start of every month, that it is time for me to go and Google myself again on the Internet and see if anything about me comes up. To speed up finding anything, you can set Google alerts to send you an email and let you know whenever your name or phone number or cheater details come up on the Internet. I strongly suggest you do this.

Just as your cache can give you away, your super-smart browser may also reveal your secrets. On the one occasion your wife figures out your password or that time you leave your computer on, while you go to the bathroom, you do not want to have predictive suggestions on the browser. This could mean that if she types E S C, she could have escort services pop up. There are some great programs for cleaning up traces, fragments and recent files you do not want to be found on your computer. I use CCleaner; there is even a free version.

Some people tell you that cleaning your entire browser history looks suspicious, but remember, the alternative might be to have advertisements based on your history. (How would you explain seeing ads for sexual products pop up on the next page that you open when your wife is standing beside you?) I would rather have the empty look.

While there are cheater guys who become obsessive and insist on using VPNs and tor traceless browsers, there is really nothing you can do if your wife has a computer expert install spyware or key loggers on your computer. These programs keep track of everything you do and report back to her later. If your spouse is at that level, she already knows that you are cheating, and is just looking for additional evidence.

Do not let her catch you by walking up behind you and looking over your shoulder.

Many men are caught because their suspicious behaviour when their wife interrupts them using their computer at home arouses her concern. Everyone has had the experience of looking at something you should not be watching, like porn and your wife walks in the room. There is that mad scramble to shut down or minimise the page you are looking at. You hear her coming up the stairs, and wonder "Do I kill the sound first or the picture? I do not want her to hear before she reaches the study door, but if she sees this, yikes!" You get the idea. Some guys even keep a mirror on their desk, so they will notice if their wife approaches from behind.

The only way to deal with this is to be permanently ready. Do not have lots of browser tabs open with revealing names sitting on the tabs of pages you thought you had quickly minimised or closed. Instead, make it so that you can shut down what you were watching with just one adjustment. Practise this until you are sure how to do that: for example, Alt F4 on a Windows computer. This is no different from what many people do at work. I once had a colleague who kept a spreadsheet sitting open on the computer desktop. When he did not want the boss to see that he was online shopping, he quickly switched to his spreadsheet with Alt-Tab. I have even seen the case where someone has a picture of a spreadsheet as their screen-saver, and on a Windows computer, a quick Windows key + L not only locks and password protects the machine but displays that spreadsheet.

As inconvenient as it is, all the history and privacy settings should be set to be cleaned out automatically. Whenever you delete files you never want to see again, you should also empty your trash folder, or better still have it set to empty every time. You do not want your wife to be able to hand you a jar with a tight lid to open while she reaches down and clicks on what you have just been browsing.

A special warning about photos

Photos are great evidence, but in your case, that evidence can be used against you. Try to avoid any and all photos. Just say no. Do not take photos, try to limit any photos your lover might take, and try and turn away or stay out of other people's photos. Avoid TV cameras and sporting events where photos and video are often taken without your knowledge.

So many men say, "I just want to have one or two sexy photos of her". For cheaters, it does not matter whether the photos of your girlfriend are bedroom shots or whether they are a snap of her smiling in the office. Why are they even on your phone? One solution cheaters use is installing one of those hidden photo vault apps. This will protect you if you can remember to use your secret vault and delete all other instances of a pic (such as the message used to send it to you, your camera's app storage or your trash folder). But how do you explain why you have the vault app in the first place? The better answer is just to avoid photos and keep your memories where they belong, in your mind.

If you are ever going to use photos in any kind of dating or arrangement site, make sure that you take your profile pics in an unidentifiable location (or mask the background). It also makes sense to remove any identifiable features like tattoos. Those tell-tale signs will make somebody sure it is *your* photo when otherwise they would not even have considered it was you. Even blurring your face is not entirely foolproof. Modern facial recognition software is powerful. If it is crucial to you to advertise yourself with an online pic but maintaining privacy is upper-most important, (for example, if you are a politician or religious leader), consider using specialised masking software such as Fawkes to make your face less computer recognisable in a profile picture.

Covering Your Real-World Tracks

Now it turns out that covering your real-world tracks is even more challenging than covering your digital tracks. This is because the environment is much harder to control.

Cars are a particular source of trouble for cheaters. First, you used the navigation system to help you find a place where you had no business being. The next time your wife is in the car, your visit comes up in the recently visited menu. You have to delete this and the dash cam. Then there is a range of parking and traffic tickets. It is always tricky when you said you were spending the day in the West of the city and a speed camera ticket gets sent to your home from a seaside village to the South. Remember to put sufficient money in parking meters so that you cannot ever get a parking ticket sent to your home with an embarrassing location. If you are heading out of town with your lover, make sure you do not fill up your car at a service station in a place nowhere near where you are supposed to be (unless you are paying cash).

Lots of cities have tolls on roads, tunnels and bridges. These are hard to avoid, but they are usually managed using an E tag or E-Z Pass system. Out of caution, you must make sure the account comes to you or is in your name. These accounts will often not only say where you were but also have the times and how often you made the trip, all nicely summarised for a month or quarter.

Do not leave anything in your car anything you do not wish to have found. Condoms, lubricants, sex toys and women's clothing are all things that people have accidentally left in their cars. When you leave them, you think, "I will take them out", then something changes. If you have such a *sex kit*, it should not be left in the gym bag or briefcase. Best if it never goes to your home.

Make sure you allow a lot of time for returning from meetings with your lover to any commitments you have made involving your wife. Like the plane delay, which leaves you in a city you are not supposed to be in, a car accident or a breakdown can be highly embarrassing when it occurs in a different place to where you have claimed to be.

When you are drunk, when you are woken from sleep or emerging from a dream are all times when you need to be careful not to call your wife the wrong name. It is a much smaller problem if you call your lover the wrong name. Elsewhere in this book, I explain the benefits of nicknames for your mistresses.

While I do not believe you should be paranoid about being seen with your lover in public, it is worthwhile limiting PDAs (public displays of affection) when you are in your home town. If you live in a very large city, you are safer than you think.

Some hobbies are great for giving you a few hours uninterrupted. Golf is great for this, especially if you explain to your wife that it is generally considered bad manners to answer the phone on a golf course, and therefore you turn it off. Just remember to take your golf clubs and shoes when you say you will be playing golf for four hours.

Cleaning up is always essential. Before you enter your home, you should always check for shirt buttons that are not aligned. It is a giveaway that you got dressed again in a hurry. Do you have hairs, lipstick marks, fragrance or glitter which should not be anywhere on you? Do you smell of perfume or sex? Of course, a deliberate tiny fuel spill while filling up your car will cover up any smell and give you a reason for a long shower, but don't start a fire!

Many men are caught out because they suddenly have a shower as soon as they get home. This is always suspicious. These guys are worried their wife will smell another woman on them, and yes, she will. Freshening up and having a shower is a great idea, but you should do this before you get home. Go via a gym and shower there, shower at your girlfriend's place, or if you use a hotel, shower before you leave it. Swimming as a fitness regime has the advantage of always leaving you with a lingering chlorine smell that covers up pretty much everything else.

Some wives are justifiably paranoid. If you are married to one of these women, things will be tricky. These are the women who will engage a private detective to follow you around. These are the same women who aim nanny cams at your desk, to look over your shoulder at your computer. Some set up a cam in your bedroom to see if you take a lover there during the day. Unfortunately, there is little you can do to protect against this because ultimately, you will want to meet up with your lover or message her, and unless you have a level of skill that comes with having worked in intelligence services, you may well be caught out.

XI.

Lift Your Game

Lots of you will consider this the most boring chapter of this book. But I would not be helping you in your quest to enjoy beautiful women in your bed if I did not cover this important area.

If you are anything like me, when you were much younger and in the dating scene looking for a partner or potential wife, you exercised, cared about how you dressed and put effort into how you looked. When you consider that being young, you probably already looked great, but you made an effort anyway, you would have been in fantastic shape back then. All of us know what it's like to look at a woman who's been married for ten or twenty years who has just "let herself go". Well, from the girl's point of view, that's what she thinks when she looks at us - "that guy has let himself go", and she's right.

You're probably carrying too much weight, drinking too much beer, and wearing old clothes. Even worse, do you get your hair cut as often as you should? Do you care about your eyebrows, and are you always properly shaved when you go out?

If you want to attract a new girlfriend who will hang on to your every word and take care of you in bed, you are going to have to lift your game. This chapter is all about self-care and making yourself both look the part and feel the part. You never know when the opportunity will arise to meet your next lover, so lift your game every time you walk out your door.

A huge side benefit is the confidence that you will get from this, and nothing is sexier to a woman than a confident man.

Although you *can* get a girl no matter how you look and what you wear, you will be far more successful long-term if you lift your game. Not only will you attract more women, but you will give your lovers a reason to stay with you when you can't give them something else that the perfect boyfriend could. So when your mistress is thinking, "I'm sure he's up to something, I don't see him as often as I'd like", you also want her to be thinking you're the best catch she's had and that she is lucky to get any of your time.

Exercise

Most of us need an excuse to do some exercise. It's about time you started. You will feel better, perform better in bed and of course, you will look more attractive to a partner. The time to start is *now*, even before you have your mistress or sugar baby. When that is the only flag, your wife will be ok with it. Once you are cheating, she may occasionally wonder about other clues— you need to limit the number of reasons she has to be suspicious at any given time.

Girls intrinsically understand body shape in a way that men do not. Even the fat girl knows she is fat, and the skinny girl knows she is thin. Most fat married guys do not know they are overweight; they think they are normal. To be honest, of course there are fat men who get loads of female attention, but it's easier if you're thin! Improving how much you weigh and what you look like naked is a combination of two things: You have to eat less and exercise more. Sounds easy, doesn't it? But the multi-billion-dollar diet industry is founded on none of this being as easy as it seems. What you need to do is find motivation.

XI | Lift Your Game

Twenty-five-year-old girls have beautiful motivational phrases like "nothing tastes as good as skinny feels". So what you need to do is find a motivator, affirmations and phrases that will make you start exercise each day or take that next step when you are tired and bored on your run. We are looking for the motivation that will make you go to the gym, swim another lap, volunteer to walk your kid's dog or continue for another 15 minutes on a treadmill. Try as motivation "I will get laid more and I will have better orgasms". It works for me!

Gyms can be a great spot for the cheating man for lots of reasons. Gyms will give you an additional place to clean up and freshen up before going home; they can also be the perfect excuse for where you were at any weird times that your wife couldn't find you. Choice of which gym is always tricky. It's a balance between one that motivates you, one where you might meet women and one that your wife will never choose to join.

If the gym is not for you, the range of ways you can exercise now is vast. There are audiobooks, podcasts, YouTube videos and many different exercise apps. Remember, if you devote some time to exercise, you will improve your muscle control, which means better orgasms. In addition, you improve your blood flow, which means better erections, and exercise that involves weights can only improve your testosterone, which helps stop you from looking like an old man when you're still young.

Diet

You are what you eat. There are easy ways to start improving your diet. In most football codes, when you can play the ball entirely unopposed, you would call that a free-kick. For you and me, diet products are our free-kick.

Start ordering the light, skim, low-fat, no sugar or diet versions of all your food, sodas, coffees, milk, creams, cheeses, and any other meal you can. Just start today. While we're getting good at this, we both know you can give up eating fast food and candy bars.

What you need to do as well as eat healthily, is eat less. Smaller portions are the way to go. Try eating two or three slices of pizza, not the whole pizza.

It is also vital to eat green vegetables. I know there are lots of you reading this who would look at a salad and say that's not food - that's what food eats. But go ahead and look after your body; vegetables are not only good for you, but they will also fill you up, so you eat fewer other things that are not so healthy.

Oh, and by the way, alcohol is full of calories! Reduce drinking and see the weight fall off you. Especially if you drink a lot of alcohol, remember to take your vitamins.

Now all that is left for you to do is step on the scales regularly to see how you are going. It is not magic, but it works.

Dentists and Dental hygienists

Over time, Hollywood has won the war when it comes to expectations of your smile. People expect pearly white teeth. This is especially difficult if you smoke or drink a lot of black coffee. These things stain your teeth, and over time your teeth move to a darker brown, and you do not notice it unless you are standing next to someone who has just had their teeth whitened.

There are various methods of addressing this, from whitening toothpaste to home whitening kits, or even better, just having a dentist whiten them occasionally. Of course, that takes money. I have friends and clients in different parts of the world who take vacations for cheap dentistry to places like the Philippines or Mexico. This can be worth considering as it is far more affordable; just make sure you get a referral to a professional from someone you trust.

It is also essential that your teeth, gums and mouth stay healthy so that you do not have bad breath. (This way, you will always taste good when you kiss your lover). You are an adult now, so you really should be getting your teeth checked by a dentist once or twice per year and even more frequently seeing a dental hygienist. If you are not used to this, a hygienist is usually a young woman who sits down and cleans your teeth from every angle using appropriate tools. Your teeth will feel great afterwards, and your breath will be fresh.

Don't forget, just like your grandmother taught you when you were a kid, you should always brush your teeth multiple times per day, preferably with an electric toothbrush; remember to floss every day and use a good mouthwash. All these things will make you far more appealing to women in ways you did not even know. Thank me later.

See your doctor

Yes, most men hate to do this, but you are all grown up now, so you can and should go and see your doctor just for a check-up. That's how people discover if they have serious illnesses in time to get them cured. Later in this book, I cover occasions you might need to visit a doctor, you should see a doctor regularly, especially if you haven't exercised for a long time.

Meditation

Just as exercise can be great for your mind - so can meditation. No, I am not going to get religious. But meditation and mindfulness can be simple; just use a smartphone app like or *Headspace* or *Calm* or one of the many podcasts. In addition, mindfulness has the great benefit of helping you stay level-headed when dealing with the stresses which come from juggling the demands of your multiple bed partners.

Fashion

"My son has followed fashion since he was a punk. He and I agree that fashion is about sex."

-Vivienne Westwood *(fashion designer, her son founded lingerie line, Agent Provocateur)*

A sad fact of life is that most straight men are not great at fashion. Men in their 30s, 40s and 50s are the worst. We all think we know what looks good. In truth we don't. The average teenage girl knows more about what looks good by the time she is 14 years old than the average man will learn in his life. Remember, women put hours, if not days, into shopping for clothes and spend lots of time getting ready for dates. If you do even a fraction of that, you will be so far ahead of most men that your success rate will soar.

In *Mad Men*, that award-winning New York TV series featuring advertising agencies of the 60s and 70s, the married advertising executive Don Draper always managed to get all the girls he wanted. Draper wasn't a particularly nice guy, but he was not shy to talk to girls, and he was always the best dressed. Now you may not look like Draper, but there

XI | Lift Your Game

is no doubt you can dress so that girls are far more likely to be interested in you.

An excellent place to start is to ask someone. The best person to ask is a woman slightly younger than your wife. (Your wife is likely to suggest fashions just a little older than you would need to wear to maximise success in your search for your next side chick.) If at all possible, get a stylist. Most of you won't wish to spend the money or be brave enough to get a stylist, but it is a great idea. You can usually get a stylist by going to a major department store and asking about a personal shopper (if you have the budget for that - try it- you won't regret it). You can also search online and easily find a stylist to help you. The budgets range from cheap to Hollywood, but they *all* know a lot more about clothing than you.

There are three aspects to what you should be wearing:

What is stylish, up-to-date, and fashionable now?
What looks good on you?
What can you afford?

Look closely at your websites, store catalogues, TV commercials, and current movies, all of which suggest fashion approaches you can take. Whatever you do— don't copy what your married forty-something-year-old friends are wearing or ask their advice. What they are wearing will be about work or for socialising with *married* people.

One year, as part of a work corporate bonding event, instead of the usual go-kart racing or mini-golf, the office secretaries and personal assistants sent our team of forty and fifty-year-old male managers to a group personal shopping experience at a major department store. They sent photographs of us and some of our sizes ahead of time. While we were sitting around eating and drinking beers and champagne, the stylists brought us items that they thought would be appropriate for us. I was horrified. I don't think I ever felt more uncomfortable. I felt stupid; the clothes that were suggested for me didn't seem right. They were expensive, and I wished I had never gone to this event. I was so happy when it was over. Then a funny thing happened...

During the next three weeks, I received more compliments on how I looked than I had received in my previous forty years added up together. It seemed as though I was on a candid-camera style TV show and I had been set up. Of course, what had really happened was that the stylist understood what would look good with my body type and skin colour, so she chose clothes for me that worked. Most importantly, the clothes made me look fantastic. I still haven't had the courage to go back to the stylist, but I have tried to choose clothes based on appropriate fashion rather than my out-of-date opinions.

You can buy online to save money. You do not need to have ten new outfits; two or three great date outfits is plenty to get you going. If in doubt, get fewer items that look better and cost a little more, rather than more clothes that look just ordinary.

Underwear is important, but since you are a man, that means that it should never appear to be a big deal. Unless you are an underwear model, or you can put them on three minutes before undressing for a girl, so they show no marks, give up on your tighty whities. Instead, decide the type of shorts you want to wear and buy a whole lot. I typically buy a go-to brand like Calvin Klein whenever I see a sale. I buy ten pairs at a time and then do not think about it.

Women wear lingerie because they want us to notice it, but we want to take it off. As a man, you should wear underwear that she hardly even notices. The worst thing is if she notices

XI | Lift Your Game

old, worn, ill-fitting underwear. By the way, any time you get to the stage of a date where you see a woman's underwear, and it is pretty lingerie, you can rest assured that she wanted to go to bed with you before you even went out on the date. However powerful you think your powers of seduction on the night were, she was ahead of you and thought it might happen.

Go ahead, throw old things out of your wardrobe and get some new clothes. What every woman knows, but sadly most men do not understand, is that new clothes not only make you look good-they make you feel confident and special. It is that confidence that gets you laid. So start now, and your wife will be enjoying the compliments from her friends about your new look, rather than wondering what is going on later when you have your new lover and are making your wife suspicious about other things at the same time as you are changing wardrobe.

Shoes

I know that none of you wants to read about shoes. The only thing you need to know is that if a girl sees a man with serious shoes, she will think he is a serious man. Make sure they are clean (polished if that is appropriate) and that they fit with the rest of what you are wearing.

XII.

Your Grooming

Hair - on your head

Women looking to attract a man go to the hairdresser frequently. They spend hundreds of dollars and many hours in the stylist's chair. The good news is you don't have to do this. However, that does not mean that it is acceptable for a man to have hair like you are in a hippie musical. Long hair went out in the seventies. Beards can look good on men in their twenties but rarely if you are older than that. There are virtually no men in positions of power who wear moustaches. Since going to the barber is cheap - get your hair cut. Have it cut short and see the barber every three or four weeks. (No- not three or four times per year.) Tell your barber you would like a neat and tidy haircut. It doesn't have to look like you just joined the Marine Corps, but above the collar and the ears is a good start. While you are there, have him trim your eyebrows. It takes him 30 seconds and believe me; it is so much easier than trying to do this yourself.

Since in most cities the average barber shop costs the price of three beers or five cups of coffee (or that takeaway meal - which you really should not be eating now you are thinking about your diet), you have no excuse not to visit your barber. What matters is not your choice of hairstyle but that you

XII | Your Grooming

look well-groomed. Once you get out of your teenage years or twenties, it is the neat and tidy guys who get laid. Right about now, some of you are saying, "don't struggling artists with beards and long hair get laid?" Let's be honest-from a woman's perspective, if you do not fix your hair, you are not an interesting artist— you are just a guy who doesn't put any effort into looking neat and tidy.

Men can and do colour their hair. You don't have to go to a salon, men's hair colour is cheap at the supermarket and quick - just a few minutes in the shower. (I can only guess why similar products for women take several times as long - perhaps they are better for your hair, but men lack patience.) Sadly, dyeing your hair often with home kits yourself will damage your hair, and over the course of time, it will make it thin and brittle. However, your hair will recover if left alone, so occasionally, when you are not going to see your lover (like when you are on a family vacation), let your hair go natural for a while. You could also visit an expensive hair salon and ask for advice or treatment.

Hair colour is one case where you should not be secretive with your wife because she will know. So casually introduce the subject to your wife and talk with her about colouring your greying hair. Make it part of a talk about getting old and needing to keep up at work or in your career. In my experience, a lot of wives say "No don't", that is a reason you *should* do it. (Tip - it doesn't help to point out that she's probably been colouring her hair for years to look attractive but doesn't want you to try it).

Hair everywhere else - where it does not belong

It is a sad truth for men that as you get older, hair disappears from your head but starts to grow everywhere else. The most typical places where hair is a problem are your ears and your nose. Most men are not even aware of this, but if you are trying to attract lovers, it creates three problems: Number one, it suggests you do not care. Two, it reminds her you are older. Three, it stops you from being the man she can dream about. Why not be that guy who is just what she wants in this area? It is simple to achieve.

If you go to a shaver store or even some large department stores, you can buy those small hand-held battery-powered hair clippers for about $10. There are about the size of a banana - you switch them on, and a little blade spins safely inside a case. You can use these to cut hair in your ears or your nose. Believe me; this is much easier than scissors. Who would have guessed that scissors in your nose and ears are not a good idea? No, not even those tiny blunt scissors, supposedly for the purpose.

Of course, if you are truly a modern guy it has become fashionable to get your nose and ear hair waxed - see the section below on waxing. Still, the aestheticians (which is the fancy name for waxing girls) tell me that it is a lot less painful than having your manzilian wax.

I do not know whether it has been five years, ten years, or forty years since you were married but believe me, things have changed in the dating world and so have the expectations of younger single girls. This is particularly true when it comes to grooming. When I was a young guy, I did not even know one man who shaved his groin. Now almost all young women seem to groom themselves "down there", and here's the secret, more and more *men* do as well. The fashion these days is either waxing or shaving. If you do not believe me, go online and search for male waxing in your area, and you will be amazed. Manscaping is a booming business.

Now while you wince in imaginary pain and start thinking

XII | Your Grooming

to yourself, "No, not me. I could not possibly", let me tell you there are alternatives. The most obvious option is shaving. Yes, you can shave down there, but it isn't easy. If you insist on this, you can do it carefully in the shower. It can be itchy, things can go wrong, and the hairs grow back quickly. A much better bet is waxing. It sounds crazy, you think, I could never do that. Or, only women or gay guys would do that. Let me tell you that since I started, I have never looked back. I always choose a woman aesthetician to do my waxing. Although it is not a sexual environment at all (imagine stretching skin and wax being pulled like a band-aid), I still cannot imagine having it done by a man.

It hurts for about three minutes, then you feel great, and here is the secret that no one tells you: You will *look* much bigger where it matters. Because you are so clean and tidy, women (yes, these modern women you will be spending time with,) find it a lot easier to be modern and friendly with you in all those places you have just taken care of. The payoff is amazing. You will want to thank me the next time you get a more positive and far more intimate reaction than you ever expected from someone pretty.

In one of my recent Executive coaching sessions, a man asked me whether he should get laser treatment. When I stopped laughing, I explained that I thought I was pushing things by recommending waxing. If you wish to explore more serious options like permanent laser, you are on your own.

If you are still sexual with your wife, to the extent that she is getting up close and personal with your private area, you will have to move to your new look gradually by shaving more and more. If you are past that point of intimacy with your wife, if the subject comes up you can talk about being sweaty and wanting to be neat and tidy, but in all probability, she will simply not notice.

Manicures

Now, this is another one that scares a lot of men. Get a manicure. Summon up some courage and walk off the street into one of those busy nail salons that exist in every large city and are usually staffed by rows of Chinese or Vietnamese girls. The remarkable thing is the staff will not look at you like you are weird, the price is cheap and you can take it from me, getting a manicure will not make you gay. You certainly don't want to be bothering with appointments and such - it's only nails. When the girls ask you what you want, just say that you want a quick manicure. They will know what to do. You certainly do not need polish, colours, or any other ridiculous things (we all know these look great on pretty women, but they will not on you).

Unlike cutting your hair, this is one which you can do yourself. Use a clipper and then a nail file and do them regularly. Even if you decide to clip your nails yourself, it is still worth making that trip back to the salon every couple of months to get a manicure. Those Vietnamese girls will take care of the shapes and the cuticles. If you're lucky, they give you a hand and forearm massage that will put a smile on your face for half the day, even though nothing even vaguely sexual happened.

Fragrances

It is always important to be careful with fragrances, aftershaves and perfumes, both yours and your new girlfriend's. Don't get me wrong; they smell fantastic. They can keep you in a girl's mind, and they can certainly hold her in your mind. There is a particular Gucci fragrance that I come across every year or two, which instantly takes my mind to the girl I once

XII | Your Grooming

dated who wore it. She stays in my head for days afterwards. The more expensive perfumes are, the longer they seem to last. Fragrances can however get into your clothes and your hair. Wives can smell them just like people can smell cigarette smoke on a smoker. (As a teenager, I used to tell my mother I didn't smoke. I realise now how ridiculous that was since my mom washed my shirts.)

Try to avoid spending time with women who wear *too much* perfume. The best advice for you is to wear just a little of an appropriate fragrance yourself. Do not go overboard; you want your date to catch just a hint of something special. Wearing the same fragrance all the time yourself can help — it can mask hers. But if you wear something strong, you may not even realise that her scent is in your hair or clothes once you become accustomed to your cologne. If you can wash up after seeing her, do it.

Men always ask me for suggestions on fragrances that they should wear when meeting women for the first time. Of course it is a very personal thing (you should test first), but some suggestions include:

If you are over 30 try Terre by Hermès.
If you are under 30 try La Nuit de l'Homme by YSL.

Almost all men look better when they have just shaved. But despite cosmetics companies marketing aftershave products that are actually fragrances (these are the ones that sting your face), the best aftershaves for your face are usually the creamy ones. If in doubt, use a men's fragrance separately from your aftershave and put a good moisturiser onto your face (and hands) after you shave. Your skin will look younger.

Remember the biggest grooming and presentation tip men should learn from women: Always look at a mirror before leaving your house — Always!

XIII.

Fun Dates

"I believe in sex on a first date. Otherwise, how do you know if a second date is worth the effort?"

-Jacki Weaver

Always make sure you have fun dates – enjoy yourself. Remember, you managed to get a girl to marry you at least once – it's been a while, but you can be still good at this dating game. It is however, equally important not to waste your time, especially while finding your next lover. Just like salesmen check out potential buyers beforehand to make sure they are not wasting their time, you should only have actual dates with girls you have previously qualified. Whether you are meeting girls in person or online, you want to have a good idea ahead of time that the girl is interested in you, before wasting a lunch or an evening having a date. You should have covered this idea in some of this book's previous chapters on meeting women before you get to this point. If haven't had a date in a while, like most of the men reading this book or attending my courses, consider this a refresher: When you are dating new women as a married man, you want to have some specific goals in mind:

XIII | Fun Dates

Having fun is half the fun!

Decide pretty quickly if she is the right sort of girl for you, or else wrap it up politely.

Subtly make sure that she knows you do not need her, or the date, but you are fun, interesting, and confident.

Make sure she is up for sex (and have some physical or intimate component like a kiss).

If all is good, get her to agree to your next catch up.

Before we go any further, men often ask me, "Should I be having sex on this date?" I have no problem whatsoever with sex on a first date. But my best, longest-lasting love affairs have been with women where I had sex on the second date. A paranoid buddy of mine always says he never has sex on the first date but waits for one or two more dates because he never hears of people being accused of fake rape charges on the second date. I find this a little extreme, but his point is well made.

If I am travelling and having a date with a woman out of my city, I usually move things to the sex on the first date. On the other hand, if I am having a date with a woman who lives in the same city as me (even if she thinks I do not live there), I know I am going to be able to see her more regularly. In these cases, and when I am looking for a longer-term side chick, I usually wait till the second date; there is something special about that for the girl:

It reinforces that you are not needy (although on the first date, you must come across as sexual, not like an older brother or someone begging to be put in the friend zone).

It makes her feel somewhat safer, and feeling safe is particularly important for women.

It allows the tension to build up for both of you.

Later, after you have slept with her on the second date, you can find a way to mention that you waited and explain that you wanted to be certain and make a virtue of it.

In the world of extramarital affairs, I cannot imagine why any guy would wait for more than two or three dates before sleeping with their new partner. Remember, if your affair is going to work, it needs to work the way you want it to. Starting at your first date, you must be setting the ground rules.

Planning dates

You are the man; planning dates is always your responsibility. Do not say things like, maybe would you like to go out sometime; be confident and always suggest an actual time and place to her. Remember always to do what you say you will do. Modern women love integrity. The really good news for you is that most girls are used to terrible dates, especially younger women, and yours will seem fantastic in comparison.

Just like when you are initially attracting or interesting a woman, at a date you need to be well presented. Look at yourself in the mirror before you go out, especially if you are rushing from work. If she does not already know you are married, take off the wedding ring. There is rarely anything wrong with wearing a suit. If you want to seem more casual, no tie, and you can always take off your jacket. Women go to an incredible amount of effort to get ready for dates. If you think that some of the advice on grooming and presentation in this book seems like a lot of trouble, it is nothing compared to what any girl would do.

At the date, when you see her, to put her at ease, stand up, smile, and look at her (but do not undress her with your eyes at the start of the date, she will find that creepy.) Tell her something simple like, "Lovely to see you, you look great in that dress". Do not make it sleazy by saying something like "your breasts look beautiful in that low-cut dress". Lots of compliments are not necessary but repeat her name so you don't forget it, and she knows that you know it.

All girls notice things – and you should also notice something about *her* that you can mention in the future or comment upon later. These should be little things, like a pair of earrings. You are looking for anything that will not seem creepy. Believe me, girls do appreciate men who notice things and remember things about them later.

Where for a first date?

A first date does not have to be overly extravagant, but you should still be a gentleman– be on time, listen, smile – get the check. Yes, without making a big deal of it, pay for dinner or drinks like it is the most natural thing in the world. (Or pay when she cannot see, like during a visit to the restroom). Walk her to her car – offer a coat if it is cold – yes really, even in this post-COVID world. Even when you are on a planned date, it never hurts to throw in something spontaneous. For example, "wow, look at that mime juggling in the square, let us go over there and see".

It is great to have restaurants that give you a home-court advantage. A place where you are known, that your wife does not go to, and the staff will not blink an eyelid about you being with a different date every time you go there. You will already know the menu, making it easy for you to be confident and suggest dishes to her (and then you can do all the ordering after she has chosen.) "The lady will have..."

There are fun things you can do to lighten up a first date. I love to use text messages during a date. If you are going to the restroom and you see her pick up her phone, or if she takes her phone to the restroom- using the number you use for messaging lovers, quickly send her (or have preset and ready to send) a text message like this:

> I am so enjoying having lunch/dinner with you. If that is the riot squad you're calling on your phone or just texting your BFF to make up an excuse to leave, can you tell her to wait another twenty minutes - I liked the look of the dessert menu.

Date conversations

Conversation will be easier if you remember a few tips. Keep it light and fun. You are interesting enough. Sit up with your back straight, look at her and smile. If you feel yourself getting nervous, imagine you are sitting with an old friend or your sister. There are all sorts of topics you can raise. I like to start laughing about some of the terrible dates I have had and hopefully she will come out with some of hers in response. You are now looking good because she is comparing you to hopeless guys in her mind.

Some men do not talk at all on the first date, but the bigger problem is that too many guys will not shut up. Let her talk. I believe a girl can talk herself into love with you. Ask questions as she talks about herself. Ask about her taste in guys. What sort of guys does she usually date? This is the sort of question you can steer towards sexual tastes if the conversation is flowing that way, but make sure you are not creepy.

It helps to sound like you are genuinely interested and that you listened to what she just said. Respond to prove that you have been listening. If she is talking about her sister, you should say things like, "I can tell that you have really put a

XIII | Fun Dates

lot of yourself into helping your cousin, you must truly care." Ask her what is important in her life. If you know something about the things that interest her, it is always good for her to see you as an expert.

If the conversation about her is still going nowhere, you can change the subject to talk about things that make you seem interesting, like your ambitions for the future— sound passionate about the things you say that you want to do.

Always be nice to people serving you. You are the man who is friendly to waiters, bartenders, cleaners and parking attendants. You always tip. Do not make apologies or excuses for yourself at any time; that makes it hard for her to see you as desirable.

On first dates, like on any date, there is a tiny chance you will be recognised. The only way to behave is to take it in your stride. For the sake of both the person who has seen you and your date, you have to act like it is no big deal. A simple "Hi, great to see you; this is Susie." You can then quickly get back to paying attention to your date. You just want your date to think that you are an important and likable guy, so of course you will know people wherever you go.

It is critically important that you are physical with her during the date, so you get to find out her response to you. (You are here for a sexual relationship after all). Early on in the date, touching her hand or her arm gently at an appropriate moment is a start. As the date progresses, perhaps moving her hair or getting her chair and reaching for the small of her back. If you are not going to proceed to sex on the first date, you must find a reasonably quiet spot (once again not creepy) and kiss her. Really kiss her; you are not talking about a peck on the cheek. For me, the woman's response to this kiss is the only thing that determines whether or not she gets a second date.

Fun dates

Here are some fun date ideas. Many of these are most suitable for future dates where you want to have fun with her, while she remembers that you are lively, interesting, and unique. Not many relationships can be sustained on meetings just for sex unless it is a clear, friends with benefits arrangement and she is getting some benefit. (Like some of her college fees paid).

Although there is nothing wrong with dinner and drinks, here are just a few examples of more unusual dates. You should always choose and then tell her what the two of you are doing. After you have been seeing her for a while, she might suggest something, but if she does, take it on board and still go with your ideas, don't feel you must jump or rush at her plan. You are in charge here; you are the man.

Trivia nights. These are great if you are clever or have excellent general knowledge because this type of event will make you look good. Often held at a bar, or even better, sometimes for a charity fund-raiser, they are cheap and fun dates, especially once alcohol is involved.

Wine tasting. This can be a class, a wine bar, one of those painting classes or even better, a trip to a vineyard. If budget is not an issue, helicopter wine tasting in a wine region is unbeatable. Knowing something about wine - starting simply with which types of wines you like and which types she might like - is never a bad thing when dating women. It adds to her perception of you as confident and exciting, and if you are not careful, you might learn something useful on these sorts of dates.

Art galleries are always great, especially if you have a ticket to some event or guided tour. The added advantage of an event is that not only do you seem cultural and connected,

XIII | Fun Dates

but an event, class or tour will only go for a finite amount of time. You do not want to be in a gallery for hours on end, that is for certain, but you also do not want to be the man who says, okay we have seen one painting; let's go to bed now.

The sorts of places you should not be going on dates, especially early in the relationship, are theatres, movies, or concerts. These will simply take up hours of your time and you are not getting to know her, or whether you even want to. Instead, you are looking at a stage or a screen. On the other hand, if you actually love these things and do not get to do them often enough, then take her for fun once you know her quite well. Consider it something of a reward for both of you.

Going to multiple places on one date, especially if she's young, can make her feel like she already knows you and therefore more inclined to have sex with you. Do not be racing across town, but it can be a good move to go to a different place for a coffee after, or a cocktail. If you are on a roll and are getting on exceptionally well, do not break up the momentum; just go to whoever's place is easiest, yours, hers or a hotel, and enjoy what comes next.

It is your responsibility if dates do not work out. Once again, you are the man. It is your fault if the restaurant or bar is closed or does not have a table for you. It is your fault if you end up without any condoms. It is your fault if you have nowhere you can sleep with her if it comes to that point. Do some planning; it will usually pay off.

Double dates are usually too complicated. Dating is not a team sport, but there are a couple of exceptions. One: it is never a bad thing if you are a manager to be spotted by somebody from work who thinks you are important. This social proof will impress your date. The second exception is the wing girl. She is a totally trustworthy female friend who knows what you are up to. Being with a female buddy will always help you seem like a decent guy to all the other girls around.

Men also ask me should they give a woman flowers or gifts on a date? No! This just comes off as desperate and needy. It is far too much for a first or second date, and she will run a mile. These super romantic ideas are best kept for her birthday (and after you have been sleeping with her a while).

XIV.

Venues for trysts

Your place or her place?

If your lover knows you are married, there will be times when you will be tempted to sleep with her at your own house or apartment. This is always risky. I have done this when my wife was either visiting her family or away for work a few days. I have enjoyed it a lot, but you should be aware that it is problematic.

Straight away, your lover will know you are married. There will be signs all over the place: from wedding photos to the women's clothing in a wardrobe, makeup in the bathroom, to those little touches which could never be in a bachelor pad. If she already knows you are married, then your place becomes a more realistic option.

One big problem is that women notice things more than men. You already know this. Think of when your wife walks into your home and says, "this place is such a mess". You think it looks fantastic because you just tidied it up. Your wife is not making this up; she is a woman and just sees things differently from you.

Your wife will notice if you have changed the sheets. She will also notice if you have not, but they have been slept in. She will find hairs on the sheets or in the laundry. She will discover that stray earing, which was left there (perhaps deliberately), or that broken fingernail. She may smell the scent of another woman or another woman's fragrance. Your wife will even smell whatever spray you used to cover up the other girly scent in your bedroom. Then there is the bathroom. Can you imagine your wife finding a feminine hygiene product wrapper or a condom in the trash?

What is worse, a neighbour may see you coming or going at an unusual time with a new woman, mention this fact to your wife and now she has confirmation, not just suspicion.

Her place is always a better choice. The problem is that as a grown man, it is tough to steer the conversation to a move to her place, especially if she has just indicated she is willing to come back to yours. Everything was ready and now she wonders, "oh, are you just cheating? Will I even see you again?"

One of the best things about her place is that you can just leave. You do not have to find a way to kick her out. If you are finished, if you are not happy, if she discovers you are married and you did not tell her, whatever the reason, you can decide how long to stay.

Love Nests

Every now and again in your life, things just fall into place. At one point, I had a rental apartment as an investment. My tenants moved out one day, and I was about to get a realtor to lease it when I had a second thought. What if I just kept it for my love nest? The problem was I had to make it seem as though I lived there, but after it was set up, I figured it was worth the loss of rent because I was having so much fun.

I had myself set up with everything I liked, clothes, wine, music, condoms, lubricants; you get the idea. Sadly I later had to sell the place, but I would not rule out setting one up again.

XIV | Venues For Trysts

Hotels

If you cannot regularly meet at your lover's place - hotels are the best option. Of course, there's a considerable price range, but that's not usually the problem. With hotels, you need to give your lover a reason that you are there and not at your place. This is especially true if your lover is a new partner. Since people are not travelling so much in these post-COVID days it is harder to explain you "are out of town" or "working in several cities". But even if you need to explain you are travelling or married (or whatever excuse you dream up), it is almost always better than sneaking into your own house.

Find a hotel that works for you and stick to it. I like to see my favourite hotels as another home-court advantage in the game of extramarital liaisons. This can be a fantastic thing, whether in your own city or out of town. Even the doormen know me.

You should be aware of some hotel hacks and tips. If you like nicer rooms and suites, it is usually cheaper to ask if they have anything extra special at check-in. (Give some excuse - it's my girlfriend's birthday). If they don't say yes immediately, say you are prepared to pay an upgrade fee. A standard room plus an upgrade fee should still be less than booking a suite from scratch.

If you just want a short daytime fling, several websites also aggregate offers that top hotels make just for part of a day (so businessmen can work undisturbed). Again, you'll find them on search engines.

Make sure you check in first, before she arrives - it gets around the middle name or ID problem if you are using alternate names for your extracurricular activities, but be careful. If you are staying in an expensive hotel, it is common for a smart digital menu to come up on the room TV. Sometimes this will have your name on as soon as you walk into the room. Sometimes it will be when you switch on the TV, on other occasions a nosey girl could scroll down the smart menu to get services and check your bill. The solution here is to get in first, accept any welcome messages and turn off the TV.

In an increasing number of high-tech hotels, your name will be displayed on the hotel room phone while you're staying in the room. The only easy solution for this is simply to push the phone out of the way and put something like a towel, brochure, or hotel menu over the top of the phone before she sees it. It is unlikely she will bother moving it. This is a reminder to stick to the earlier rule; you really should check in to the hotel room first.

Lastly, some hotels like to slide a bill under your room door in the early hours of the morning of the day you check out. This has lots of risks for you if your lover sees it, not only your details (name and address) but that you are leaving town!

XV.

Bedroom Health

"Look at all the things that can go wrong for men. There's the nothing-happening-at-all problem, the too-much-happening-too-soon problem, the dismal-droop-after-a-promising-beginning problem; there's the size-doesn't-matter-except-in-my-case problem, the failing-to-deliver-the-goods problem...and what do women have to worry about? A handful of cellulite? Join the club. A spot of I-wonder-how-I-rank? Ditto."

-Nick Hornby

The bottom line, in the bedroom

It can be tricky as a mature guy going to bed with a new sexual partner. Since you're reading this book it's probably because you're a man who's been married for a while, so you may be in your forties, fifties or sixties and let's be honest here, your erections might not be what they used to be.

The other problem you might encounter while trying to get an erection is a head problem, not a physical, sexual problem. Lots of guys report that when they are first cheating on their spouse or first-time sleeping with a new woman who is not their wife, they find it difficult to get or keep an erection. This can be guilt messing with you, or it can be just the stress of a new partner and how will she judge you. Yup, good old-fashioned male performance anxiety, and you thought things were tough when you were a teenager.

The good thing about 21st-century medicine is that everything is easily fixable. Even better, if the problem was just a head problem, it's highly likely that once you get used to enjoying good sex with lots of different women again, you will find this problem goes away, and in fact, your body gets better than ever.

In most countries, you need to see a doctor in order to get Cialis or Viagra. These drugs used to be expensive, but now they are going out of intellectual property protection such as patents, and they are becoming relatively cheap.

Whatever you do, never go to one of those crazy clinics advertising "fix your impotence", instead just go to see any regular doctor. They will probably check you don't have some heart condition or other medicine that stops you from taking them before prescribing you the pills that will do the trick. Cialis works for more than a day but doesn't start working for an hour or so after you take it. In France, we used to call it *le weekend* pill because it lasts so long. On the other hand, Viagra only lasts a few hours. Cialis is sometimes prescribed for prostate concerns, so when your wife finds them - you have an excuse.

So, what do you say to your doctor? I would come straight out and say you are concerned that you are having trouble with your erections. If you are just mildly concerned and want harder erections but are worried that they are being stopped by emotional or head problems, explain to the doctor that your plumbing still works, and you know this because you can wake up with morning wood.

I have typically said to the doctor that I've been going through a trial separation with my wife, and when back together with her, it's just too stressful, and things are made worse by my inability to get it up. So the doctors typically take sympathy on me and give me lots of prescriptions.

The alternative is to try using physical methods such as a cock ring. If you have never used something like this, it all seems very strange and embarrassing. If however, there are times when whatever amazing bedroom play you want to try requires you to stay hard for an exceptionally long time, these are just the thing.

STIs - Sexually Transmitted Infections

There are some messages you never want to read on your phone. Here is the exact text message that I received out of the blue on my backup phone from an unknown number one morning.

> Hi,
>
> I am contacting you privately as I have tested positive for Gonorrhoea.
>
> This is easily treatable, and I highly recommend you get yourself tested at the earliest opportunity.
>
> You may not be positive however I would hate for you to be left unaware.
>
> Kind regards.

I was blown away. I didn't know what to think. I was scared, worried, angry, and not sure which girl it related to. A message like this is not sent directly by the girl, it is sent by a sexual health service or in some cases, a website where someone who has just tested positive for an STI (sexually transmitted infection) can put in all of their contacts and each contact will receive an anonymous message like this one to take the sting out of having to communicate.

There is no question at this point; you simply must see a doctor. So off I went to a medical clinic where no one knew me. When I told the doctor, straight away, she knew the message I was talking about and claimed that she sees them all the time. She gave me an extensive battery of sexual health tests and then treated me for gonorrhoea anyway. A few days later, all my tests came back clear I had been safe all along, but it was the wake-up call I needed.

The moral of the story is always, always, always use a condom.

Once you start dealing with different girls, you may one day expose yourself to one of the scammer types. Although it is rare in the 2020s, these are girls who will pretend to be pregnant, pretend to need money for an abortion, or pretend they have already had one, and you should pay for it. If you are sensible in following the types of girls to choose, it is unlikely that you will come across these scammers, but once again— as much fun as it is to have natural unprotected sex with your lovers, take away some worries and always use a condom. Yes, even if she says she is on the pill.

A good buddy of mine says he has never had as much fun as when a girl told him that she thought she might be pregnant, and he waited to see how her story developed. He was, of course, "the only guy it could be". But, unfortunately for her, he had not mentioned that he had the snip 18 months prior.

XV | Bedroom Health

Enjoying things your wife won't do

"The only unnatural sex act is that which you cannot perform."

-Alfred Kinsey

Affairs give you an amazing opportunity to try out all your wildest fantasies.

A few years ago, I decided to get very adventurous. So on one work trip to a city where I often visited a pretty young thing, I decided to take a "bag of tricks". If you learn one thing from this book, believe me when I tell you that there are things you only want to put into your checked baggage. Airport security seemed to get their fun for the day when they visibly drag handcuffs and restraints out of businessmen's carry-on bags.

If your wife is simply not into whatever bedroom fantasy you have wanted to try for ages (you know what I mean), whether it is dressing up or unusual acts, believe me you can find a girl on the side who is into it. This is especially true if you are dating younger women.

Provided everything is consensual, you have nothing to lose. Just remember that if you suddenly decide you like something new, you must forget about it and not try your new moves in the heat of passion when you at home with your wife (that is, if you are still even having sex sometimes with your wife.)

You should also remember that you do not want to go home with bruises, bites, a hickey or even weirder marks on places where they should not be. You must be firm with your girlfriends about this and if they do not accept your rules, end the affair there and then.

Just when you thought it was going well

I fear Greeks and those bearing gifts.

-Virgil

From my Past: Karla

Lesson - Check for gifts that turn into Trojan horses

In the Roman poet Virgil's epic about the Trojan war, *The Aeneid*, he explains that the best way is to fear those bearing gifts. A small gift once very nearly got me into all sorts of trouble. I decided to "go on a work trip" and take a couple of days at a "conference" in Hawaii. This turned out to be a fantastic vacation at a beach hotel with a gorgeous young German woman I had been seeing on and off, mainly around work conferences. After a few days filled with sunset cocktails and enough lovemaking to put a smile on my face for weeks, we caught our separate planes back to our homes.

Usually, when I return home from a trip I unpack and do my laundry straight away. On this occasion, I did not. I just tipped my laundry bag straight into the basket in my bathroom. The next day when I thought I had better do some laundry, I picked up the basket and a card fell out. It was a photo of the two of us kissing, with a huge I love you written underneath. She must have had a waiter take the picture.

It was just sheer luck that my wife did not empty the laundry basket first. I have no idea what prompted Karla to choose a secret way of declaring her love, but ever since I have been incredibly careful of Trojan horses. Common places that girls leave little messages include shoes, pockets, toiletry bags and suitcases.

XVI.

On the Road

Cheating when travelling

Let's face it, if you are going to be cheating, you may as well do it anywhere that you can. When you are away from home, an affair is easier, has more novelty and is less likely to get you caught. Just remember that things are different when you are away from home. Language can be an issue, but it has never been for me. I have had fun affairs in Russia, Portugal, Vietnam and the United States, none of which are home countries for me.

In an earlier chapter of this book, I explained that it is important for cheaters to have routines. When you are travelling and cheating, it is even more critical that you have your routines set up, this is both for your safety and simply to make things manageable.

Here are some of the routines which I use when I travel for business. I always memorise my room number as soon as I am given a room, and I say it to myself every time I look at the room door. I always put the room card in the same pocket. I never store my room number with the key. I always use the same PIN in the room safe if I choose to store valuables in it. My view is that the room safe is only of limited use against the hotel staff, but it is probably safer than leaving your bag in the room. However, an in-room safe is perfect for keeping money, wallets, passports, phones, and keys secure from that girl you do not know well who is visiting you and sleeping over. She may decide to go through your things when you are drunk or asleep or, in the worst case, if she has slipped something into your drink.

In some countries, hotel security staff are never happy about you taking an unregistered girl back to your room. You can usually find out online if a particular hotel is girl friendly or not. While hotels are better for your personal security, serviced apartments are always far more guest friendly.

Whilst I am not recommending it, I know that lots of men like to party with girls when they are travelling. Sometimes this involves substances. Just remember that in other countries, the laws are different to the ones you have at home and make sure that you do not carry anything across any borders, even accidentally.

A range of laws can be different in other countries. For example, women from the Philippines are known the world over for their beauty, kindness and attention to men. There is no shortage of guys from Western countries who travel to the Philippines to meet girls. Even in this post-COVID time, men are choosing to retire in the Philippines, not because of the climate and inexpensive lifestyle, but because it is easy for them to find a partner or side chick. It's worth remembering that technically, adultery can be illegal in the Philippines. This is also the case in several Middle Eastern countries. The moral of the story, as ever, is to do your research and be private about your fun.

XVII.

Pay to Play

Escorts

"I remember the first time I had sex - I kept the receipt."

-Groucho Marx

Pay to play just means spending money to get the sex you want. This chapter is about sex workers. Yes, they are known as escorts, hookers and prostitutes. The demimonde, as it was once called. We are all adults here; this is the oldest profession in the world and married guys looking for some excitement form the largest part of their customer base. I do not make any kind of judgement, but for me, I prefer the idea of seeing the same girl repeatedly rather than anything likely to be a one-off.

Girls involved in sex-related industries are already good at keeping secrets, doing what they are asked and not invading your space. For all these reasons, they are popular with lots of married men. In some places where it is not legal, the thought of being caught or extorted is a scary one, and some of the best escort girls require you to identify yourself to protect them from the risk of law enforcement problems. Sadly, there goes your privacy.

The impersonal nature of visiting a brothel is not suitable

for some men. (Although some men find it is ideal, because you choose a girl, spend an hour or two and leave happy, refreshed and free of any ties). It should go without saying that you should pay cash in such an establishment, even if they accept credit cards. Just remember to have an excuse for why cash came out of your accounts (if you don't have a secret fun account).

Because the business is either stigmatised in many parts of the world or illegal in others, it can sometimes be difficult to know exactly what you are getting. It is not as though your brother or your workmate is going to say to you, "Hey there is a great little blonde spinner at the nearby brothel. Her name is Jasmine, do yourself a favour and try her out."

Among the problems you will find if you regularly meet with escorts who visit you at your home, office, or hotel is the bait and switch problem. That is, the girl advertised online is not the same girl as the one who visits you. You should also add to that the fact that some of the independent girls, by their very nature, are quite flaky. They do not always show up when they are supposed to. (New sugar babies can also be flaky, so build that your plans.)

I believe the only reasonable way to see escorts is to look at reviews. All around the world, there are independent online escort review sites. These are entirely different to websites owned by escorts or simply advertising escorts. (Although some also carry paid ads). It will not be hard for you to find a guide that is the largest and best of its type in your part of the world. Obviously, this is the sort of thing for which you use a one-off or cheater email address. Sometimes they require a few dollars to be a member. For anonymity, to keep your privacy, you should just charge this kind of thing to a prepaid credit card which you can quickly and anonymously buy at a supermarket or service station.

XVII | Pay To Play

If you are the sort of man who requires something highly specialised and unusual to make you happy in the bedroom, a review site is also where you will find out which girls offer precisely what you enjoy. With reviews, you will reduce your risk considerably, and no doubt enjoy yourself.

Escorts and other sex workers have regular lives too; yes they date guys and sometimes they date clients. But it is fair to say that any girl who is in sex work for a while, puts up with a lot of rubbish from men. So your best bet of finding a girl who is fun and not too jaded for activities outside of her work is to ask someone relatively new to the business or a girl who is not yet fully committed to it.

Sugar Babies and Arrangements

"The big difference between sex for money and sex for free is that sex for money usually costs a lot less."

-Brendan Behan

Some years ago, most sugar baby or seeking sites were incredibly efficient. Now they are less so, but they still have their uses. You can find online reviews of each of them and choose the one that suits you. Unfortunately, while some are fantastic, a couple of these sites are simply scams from start to finish.

On the useful sites, there are three sorts of women:

Sugar baby type I: Professional escorts trying to look to a different market to meet some guys. Amongst the ways you can detect them is that hookers like to use stupid escort names like Ashley, Victoria, Jasmine, Tiffany, Scarlet, Roxy, and so on... you get the idea. Another way, you will tell, is just the aggressive approach they take, it seems too professional they know all the jargon and abbreviations. Most men know that any time and any place where girls seem too keen on you, something is too good to be true. In countries like the United States, these sites are popular as they try and get around the fact that most sex work is illegal in that country. In Europe, Australia, New Zealand, and other countries where prostitution is regulated, decriminalised, or legal; these sites are less likely to be used by regular prostitutes. But there will still be some working girls trying to increase their market.

Sugar baby type II: Genuine sugar baby candidates. These are regular girls who want a man to give them money or an allowance. In exchange, they will spend time with you. (Yes, they all know that will include going to bed with you, even though some pretend they do not). The amount of money these girls want varies, but it is usually less than the cost of escorts, and you are likely to get something far more like a regular date or even a girlfriend.

Sugar baby type III: Regular girls who have thought about being a sugar baby but are happy just to have classy dates instead of a guy who actually pays them money. They are tired of cheap rubbish boys, want some excitement and do not mind older guys. If you play your cards right, never bring up money and offer them experiences that they never have elsewhere; some of these girls are thrilled to share your bed and your time without any payment ever.

Membership on these kinds of arrangement dating sites does cost real money, but in my experience, if you are interested in a sugar baby, they are well worth it. Just remember to pay for your membership with a prepaid, throw away credit card to keep your anonymity. Do not sign up for an extended period until you decide that it really is for you. These sites have one huge advantage over regular dating sites. Age gaps are expected. Most traditional dating sites will not offer you

XVII | Pay To Play

matches more than ten years younger in age. On these arrangement sites, it is totally reasonable and expected that a guy who is forty or fifty will be matching with women who are in their twenties.

On these apps, you can choose your city or even select multiple cities, which is perfect if you travel or if you are going to be away on a trip and you want to have something arranged for when you get there. They are possibly the only dating websites where it is common for men to cover all or part of your face. I wear a COVID mask in mine. Before you put any photo on any website or dating app, refer to the chapter in this book on covering your digital tracks and do not use a dating photo that you use anywhere else for any other reason.

You need to maximise your chances of success on an arrangement site. Although showing your face is not critical, what you put as a profile can make all the difference to your hit rate. If you want to stand out from the rest of the guys, it is important to get a few things exactly right.

When you get to choose a username, think of something interesting which says a little bit about you, two or three words is acceptable. Do not sound the same as every other guy. If you are using photos, they should just be of you with your face partially obscured and not showing any other people. Proof-read, spell and grammar check anything you put online, whether it is your profile or a reply.

If you are replying to a girl, make it clear that you have read her profile, and you are not simply just giving her a cut-and-paste of what you always say. There can be cut-and-paste elements, but make sure you address issues in *her* profile. A girl on these sites who has almost no profile is essentially asking for you just to make an offer for a date.

Do not chase too hard! Once again, no girl wants a desperate man. Also, realise that a pretty woman may get dozens of replies, so do not take it too personally if you do not hear back from her.

If you are writing a profile or an introduction, it is important to qualify the girl. I usually say that I am looking for women of integrity who apply passion and purpose to what they do. It is best when she feels that *she* can clear some hurdle rather than you. Find a way to mention sex in your profile, like a vacation together or enjoying time to get to know one another better right *after* a romantic dinner. This is to make sure that she is not going to be a sex only comes after many dates kind of girl.

Some potential sugarbabies ask for money or expenses just for a meet up like a cup of coffee. I believe that is always a mistake. If you are prepared to pay, it should be when she agrees to spend time in your bed. Even then, you may not have to pay her at all if she is enjoying the lifestyle you offer.

Strippers

You know strippers — yes, the ones with a name which is either copied from a Disney Princess or the name of a precious stone or perhaps a month of the year. How could you not enjoy a woman named January or Sapphire? Strip clubs are fun, and lots of guys all over the world enjoy them. They can be a great place to have a night out. Even better, to my way of thinking, going to a strip club and watching girls dancing, taking their clothes off or rubbing themselves on your lap is not cheating (unless you decide to date a stripper.)

If you are not in your own city, it is best to look online or just ask at your hotel. In most cities, it is possible to find a safe strip club quickly and easily. There are some small practical problems even at fun clubs. Glitter on your clothes

XVII | Pay To Play

can be removed, but you must be incredibly careful since it gets absolutely everywhere. Strippers who use lots of glitter do not think ahead; their clients are certainly not going to be bringing them any repeat business after their wives and girlfriends realise the guys have glitter in their hair, eyebrows and wherever. An even bigger problem is fake tan. I can understand this makes the girls look better under nightclub style lighting, but it is simply tragic on a white business shirt. From my experience, you may as well throw the shirt away if she has been rubbing her pretty body all over you.

Depending on where you are in the world, you will have to watch out for clip joints. I have fallen foul of clip joints in London, Paris and Manila, and I am a seasoned traveller. These are places that try and bring in guys, get them drunk and then rip them off - usually by changing prices on them or inventing fictional bills and not letting the men leave until they have paid them. Examples include suggesting to you that the price of your drink is five dollars and after you have had two or three drinks with the girl, pointing out that the price of each of her drinks was $45. In London at one clip joint. I was quite tipsy but carefully and deliberately paid for my drinks as I went along. When it came time that I chose to leave, I was distracted by a new girl who arrived. The girl with whom I had been drinking disappeared, and a giant bouncer came and presented me again with the bill for all my drinks for the night. I held my ground that I had already paid, and it worked out okay. But you get the idea. In general, if you are taken somewhere by an unknown cab driver, the chances are you are taken to an unreliable clip joint, and your driver is getting a commission because you are being ripped off.

It is possible to date strippers. But there are problems. Firstly, these girls are used to making a significant income, so money matters to them. If they have managed to earn their living as a stripper for a while, they are incredibly good at psychological hacks to get men to part with money. Secondly, a lot of them end up in a party culture and they will party far harder than you. Whatever they say initially, of course they date guys who come to the club, but there will always be another guy asking her out tomorrow. As with escorts and other sex workers, your best bet is finding a newbie, who is not all about the business.

You will find lots more detailed information in my book *Stripclub Guide*.

Alternatives

There are many women who operate around what the French once called the demimonde. These girls are not escorts, but because of the jobs they do work in, they are already very open to all things sexual and are very accustomed to keeping quiet about their activities. The sorts of girls I am talking about are the massage girls, cam girls, and others who work in risqué occupations.

Whilst these girls are regularly propositioned, they often do not find it easy to find boyfriends or partners. Even better, their expectations of the men they date as perfect boyfriend material or prospective husbands are not very high. All of this works well for you.

If you are the sort of married guy who uses these services, flirt with these girls, treat them nicely, but firmly and ask them out. You have nothing to lose, and you are likely to be pleasantly surprised. This is especially true if they are relaxed about work versus personal life boundaries.

Use your newfound confidence. You still have a wife at home, whatever this girl says, there are lots of other opportunities - so rejection is not going to be a problem - just ask her out.

XVIII.

Keeping it going

Play by your rules

When you start to see a new girl, you have the chance to run the relationship your way using your rules. This is not your marriage, and the same rules do not have to apply.

Part of your appeal as a confident man is that she can trust you to know what you're doing - if you catch yourself explaining why you are doing things or saying sorry - stop. Guys who need to apologise all the time are not sexy. Always follow through - do what you say you will do. You must be the absolute rock. This is especially true if we are talking about much younger women.

Do not be shy to be sexual; none of us would be here if men had not slept with women in the past. When you are with your lover, it does not help to profess that you are faithful to her and pretend to be monogamous. It simply creates problems for you – once again – this is your chance to play a relationship by *your rules*. Of course, men being men, we all love the idea of having our newest conquest faithful only to us. To try and get her to be exclusively yours, lots of guys reciprocate and slip into the trap of saying, "You are the only one" and other crazy things. All that this will do is get her thinking of white picket fences or babies. It will soon move on to her pressuring you to settle down, becoming demanding and tedious, all the things you went outside your marriage to avoid. If you start with your rules, the worst thing that can happen is that she decides that the relationship you are outlining is not for her. In that case, you just move on to the next girl. Always remember that you are already married, so you are not desperate. The best thing that can happen is that she accepts that you are the man, and she is the woman, and voila, you have a relationship on your terms.

Humans can be emotional after sex; this is especially true for women but can also affect men. I have been guilty of this on many occasions. I blame human love hormones, particularly oxytocin and testosterone. They will affect your lovers, and they may affect you. Therefore, you have to be incredibly careful about what you do after sex. In most cases, once a woman has slept with you, she feels committed. This is even more so after you share the bed twice.

You can make use of this effect to have your lover primed for your next liaison, but make sure you are aware of the impact on you so that you do not start falling in love. This is often the point where married men begin to tell her their secrets. As a result, you may find you begin to do things you never intended when you first started the affair. Be careful.

As the relationship develops, remember never to panic. You are the man, nothing phases you. You must not jump at shadows or reply too quickly to her messages, and you certainly must not buy into any drama she may create. She is unconsciously trying to test you, and she will not respect you for taking seriously any pettiness she creates.

A cheater's life needs to be simple. You need to respond negatively any time she tries to create relationship drama.

XVIII | Keeping It Going

No trophies

Lots of men like to keep trophies. I have been guilty of this many times. Trophies are things that remind you of your conquests — girls who you enjoyed and the fun times you had. You are better off finding new fun than trying to keep a token or trophy to help you remember old fun that you had in the past.

Here are some examples of trophies that men keep:

That Christmas card she gave you with the sexy message written inside.
That Photo Booth pic of the two of you.
The book she gave you for a birthday present which has *all my love* handwritten in the front.
The boarding passes from the trip the two of you took together.

Do not keep any of these; one day they will be found, and you will not be able to explain them. Even worse, they are likely to be found long after the affair is over, and you could have escaped clean and free if you had not kept trophies. Finally, listen out for suspicious questions; they often follow the discovery of your trophy drawer.

From my Past: Christina the nosey girl

Lesson - Girls will snoop

Some girls are truly nosey. Christina was one of those women who pretended not to need any details about me but then went and spied on my information anyway. - I also remember that she had the most geometric newsreader style nose job. Christina was good fun and was dating me while trying to get over an affair in the office with her married boss. I had met her on a sugar baby website, but she did not want money. She suggested however, that I pay for her trips to go and visit her family interstate every month, and I was perfectly happy to do this. One day as I was booking her a ticket online, I noticed the website had changed. It asked me to put in the name of the person booking. I was reading a novel by the science-fiction writer Isaac Asimov, so I just typed his name down in the box. I went ahead and paid for her ticket with a prepaid credit card. Two weeks later, when she was back from her trip, I heard Christina call me Mr. Asimov as she slipped between the sheets and started to slide down to the bottom of my hotel bed.

Yes, she had her air ticket, but that was not enough. Christina had used it to spy on me. She must have called the airline or gone to great trouble to find my details. (I had of course previously tried the airline check-in website, and it did not give her details of the booker.) Because I had been careful, it did not matter to me, and I was a little bit too distracted at that point in time to correct her and tell her she had my name wrong.

XVIII | Keeping It Going

Staying overnight

Do not initially have her spend the night – the idea is to have a relationship on your terms. Experience shows that many women can soon start feeling that they are in charge of things or making themselves at home if you let them stay the night. Do not do this early in the relationship.

I know it is nice to wake up in the morning, turn over, smile at a pretty face, and start your fun again, but it does complicate things. Several times I have been away "on business" and enjoying breakfast in bed with a pretty young thing when my wife has called at 7 a.m.— just to catch me and update me about something before I start my day. This situation is hard to juggle unless you have your lover well-trained. Do you go out of the room to answer? To the other room if you have a hotel suite or serviced apartment? Do you go to the bathroom? Do you stay and try to talk like everything is fine while you are talking to your wife? If you do, and your lover was not previously aware that you are married, she is now, and you are asking for all kinds of trouble - possibly even during the phone call. None of this would have happened if she had just gone home late at night.

In this scenario, since at 7 a.m. there will never be a good reason not to answer your wife's phone call; the only sensible approach is to answer straight away, but explain you are at a breakfast meeting with some colleagues, and you will call her back. You can then tell your lover that your boss, brother, or someone in a different time zone has a drama (whatever fits with your stories to date). Finally, explain that you would, of course, far rather have breakfast in bed with her – so the phone call can wait.

Having a side chick stay the night poses many security problems, depending on the type of woman she is, where you met her and your level of trust, especially early in the relationship. You also do not want to have the complexity that can result from her going through your things when you are fast asleep. Of course, not *all* girls will do this, but any girl who does will undoubtedly discover some of your secrets, and the less she knows, the better it is for you. Although I confess that I sometimes will try and find out more about a girl while she is asleep, I still believe most girls won't bother to do this.

The ways to make this comfortable are to drop hints much earlier (when you know you are sleeping together), and then after making love - ask if you can arrange a car for her. Then, act like her going home is the most natural thing in the world. Do not drop hints immediately before getting into bed; feeling disposable will turn her off.

Finding time together

For a married man, it can be tough to find extended periods of time with a lover, who you have got to know well and whose company you especially enjoy. Having an hour in bed after a dinner date is one thing, but there is nothing as lovely as having some days away with your mistress. So there are two problems you have to juggle. The first one is getting the time away from your home. The second one is getting time away from your work. Guys who want to try this usually use some of their work holidays, sick or personal leave days. Fortunately, no one's wife keeps track of these accurately. It does, of course, depend on what you need to do to convince your employer that you are sick.

If I am going on a work trip or conference which lasts two days, I tell my wife I am away three or four days. I try and get

XVIII | Keeping It Going

some days out of work and spend two days with my mistress, even if it is in my home city. Some men claim they are at conferences which cover part of a weekend. I even have a friend who tells his wife he needs to visit a meditation retreat every six weeks to keep his sanity.

Romantic things you can easily do for your lover

Women love romantic gestures. They have been conditioned to, and it will not change anytime soon. Some of the most romantic things you can do for your lover are simple and inexpensive. Try this list. You will be amazed at the positive responses you receive.

Give her a name. Yes, a nickname that only you and her use. Not the sort of name that a lovestruck child would call their pet kitten, but give her a simple adult name. I find it easiest to base the name on hers. It also lets you have a unisex name in case you are overheard or in case you talk in your sleep. For example, one of my lovers was called Annika and I decided to call her Nikki. Not only did she love it, but it is a perfectly unisex name, so there is no problem if anybody hears me on the phone. Naming her also gives her a psychological reminder that you are in control.

Make a playlist. Depending on your age, you first came across playlists as a teenager on cassettes, CDs or shared on Spotify. If you are on an enjoyable date, take note of the music around you. It can also be helpful to draw attention to a couple of the songs that are playing when you are with her in a restaurant or on a date. Put these songs into a playlist and next time you are with her, have them playing on a speaker in your bedroom or hotel room. If she responds positively (or after you mention one or two of the songs), you can send her the playlist in an appropriate format. It gives her lots of opportunities to think of you.

Send her a postcard. Yes, it is old school but next time you are on a trip somewhere, mail her a card telling her you are thinking of her from where you are. This works even better if you and your lover are away on a trip together. Then, when she gets home, she will have a card from you saying how much you were enjoying your time with her. You can thank me later.

From my Past: Georgia - always the student

Lesson - Crazy can come out of nowhere

Georgia was one of those girls that you know from the start is crazy and you hesitate for a moment, but you know it's going to be fun. She was always wearing alternative fashions but not looking like a hippie. She was a student but I could see that while she was smart, she was totally disorganised. I loved that Georgia cracked jokes in several languages and read poetry.

The doormen at my favourite liaison five-star hotel absolutely loved her and would laugh about her to me when I was there without her.

Although I haven't had a cigarette since I was in college, Georgia loves to smoke but usually didn't smoke around me. One night in my hotel suite, she decided to light up a cigarette after having had lots of drinks. I explained to her that she couldn't do that. As you can imagine, it was hard for me to be serious when I was naked with a glass of champagne and a pretty twenty-four-year-old redhead displaying her body on the other end of my bed. Even in my tipsy state, it was very quickly clear that this was not going to end well. My regular

XVIII | Keeping It Going

hotel had all sorts of perks for me, and I really didn't want to spark the series of problems that would result from setting off alarms in the non-smoking hotel. Summoning my serious *older guy knows better* voice, I explained to her that there were all sorts of hotel charges and fines, a smoke alarm in the room and probably laws against smoking in hotels anyway. Georgia grudgingly put out her cigarette. She turned her body away to say without any words, in the way that only women can, that my sexual fun for the night was over.

I woke from my sleep sometime later, and when I got past my immediate panic that Georgia was not in my bed, but awake and either going through the hotel folio on the TV or my wallet in the room safe, I realised the shower was running. This was very strange as she had already taken a shower after we had sex. I realised that I could vaguely smell smoke. She was in the bathroom having a cigarette and told me that having a shower would absorb all the smoke. For those of you thinking about experimenting, trust me, it helps just a little, but it is still obvious someone's been smoking.

Georgia was that sort of girl; totally not interested in rules or norms.

XIX.

How to end an affair

All good things must end, and everyone has his favourite version of how to terminate an extramarital relationship. Even if you are a nice guy and don't want to hurt her, remember that you are a married man, and you don't need any loose ends. When it's time the affair is over, and you don't want it to become any messier, there are two useful approaches: the traditional and the modern.

The traditional way is to call her or send her a message with some version of "Thank you, but with a thousand regrets, goodbye". The benefit of this is she is not in any doubt. She knows it's over, and you're not going to enter into ongoing discussions about why it happened. (Make sure you don't!). If it's face to face, just say it and finish. Of course, she may cry or shout - stick to your guns.

The 21st-century version is called ghosting. You just stop answering and block her on your phone or messaging service. If you met her on a website or app, block her on there and leave it at that. Although this is easy to do and theoretically possible if you have been smart and thorough enough to retain some anonymity, with ghosting you do run the very real risk of sending her crazy. You do not want a woman scorned trying to track you down. For example, you do not want her contacting the website where you met her, claiming

XIX | How To End An Affair

that you are a rapist or similar; quite frankly, you just want it over! I have tried both ways with good and bad results. It is very much a judgement call.

As devious as it may sound, the main reason I always claimed to be divorced, but single rather than admitting I am married is so my lover will not try and track me down to tell my wife out of revenge if the side chick and I have a bad breakup.

Things are much more complicated if the lover decides to end it with you. Although it can be very tempting to try and stay or fix whatever the problem was, it's usually not worth it, even if it's fixable. (For example, if she claims you don't see her enough – you could see her more.) Usually, there is perfectly good a reason why you did not do whatever it is she needs done. (Let's say because you're married, or you actually live in a different city, and she doesn't know that).

If you make changes and chase after her, the power dynamic shifts considerably if you come back. She now knows she can make you change or do things. Stop and think. That's not what you want in a relationship whose only purpose is to make it possible for you to get sex on the side when you want. So, if she ends it - unless you're sure that it is simply an FWB renegotiation or something else obvious, just be super polite and say I'm sorry if that's how you feel, I do care for you and I hope things work out well for you; perhaps we can catch up in the future. And you are out of there, ready to try someone new and different with whom you can have all-new adventures. If she comes back later – don't make it easy for her.

From my Past: Karla (again)

Lesson - Just end it, before you get more Trojan Horses

Although I strongly recommend keeping your marital status secret from most of your lovers (I always claim to be divorced), sometimes it does pose risks. For example, one day Karla called my office. I had not heard from her for several months as we lived in different countries. She explained that she was at the airport, catching a flight to my city, and she did not want me to talk her out of it. She was coming "for a wedding" and she hoped "we could catch up." It was tricky to have Karla in my city; to be able to spend time with her but not have her visit my home was difficult – she expected to stay with me and then became super suspicious.

In retrospect, I should not have tried to keep juggling; I should have simply broken it off with her when I stopped seeing her regularly.

A breakup can end well

"A woman can become a man's friend only in the following stages - first an acquaintance, next a mistress, and only then a friend."

-Anton Chekhov, *The Three Sisters*

Every now and again, in the rarest of circumstances, you can break up with a lover and stay friends. The advantage of these unusual situations is that she will not only be a friend, but she can make a fantastic wing girl. And when you go out together, you will find that other women you meet trust you and are instantly closer to you. This is because they think, of course, you must be trustworthy; you have such a nice female friend with you.

You can often have your pick of women in the restaurant, bar, or party because your wing girl has given you what the experts call *social proof* of being a trustworthy guy. From the new girl's point of view, you must be safe. You couldn't possibly be a creep or a thug; you have already been vetted by another respectable woman. As a result, although the new potential lover knows she just met you, of course she can sleep with you.

I must stress that these situations do not often occur; in my life I have only had one. We meet but no longer sleep together. Anytime I catch up with my fun ex-lover, we have a great time, and I end up leaving with a different woman, usually gorgeous, whom my ex-lover has spontaneously teed up for me by secretly explaining to her that I am some kind of great catch.

XX.

How men get caught

"Women and children can afford to be careless, but not men".

-Vito Corleone in The Godfather

Six degrees of separation

The barista at my wife's favourite café moonlighted as a late-night waiter in a restaurant she went to once with her girlfriends. Happy to see her, he said how uncanny it was that he had seen me just the night before. She was upset with me because without lying, I had let her believe that I was at work. She wrongly assumed that I had been with a male friend who was particularly needy (he was getting over a marriage breakup and had been trying to have dinner with me to talk about it). My wife did not ask her barista, and the waiter didn't mention, that I had been there with a pretty date. I think he had assumed that I had a good reason to be with her.

The moral of the story is that someone knows someone, wherever you are. There will always be a risk. I have been on dates with lovers and have been interrupted by business colleagues and always find that you will do just fine provided you do not have a guilty face. The only problem comes when it is somebody who is socially involved with your wife. Many of you who have seen the HBO television show *The Sopranos*, will be familiar with the scene where gangster Tony goes to the same upscale restaurant with his mistress and with his wife two nights in a row. On the second night, the maître d' makes a point of saying to his wife how long it is since he has seen Tony, for a huge tip of course. It is always good to have a home court like that to which you can take dates. I have restaurants, hotels, and drivers, all of whom are used to getting my business and know how to keep their mouths closed.

Become a better liar

There are tricks to being a better liar. The critical thing is to practise. Think of the sorts of questions you might get asked if you are caught out or if your wife gets very suspicious. Have great answers ready for the examples below. Spend as much time as you can practising small lies to friends and colleagues, so you get much better at it. Decide what stories you will tell your wife and what you are going to say to your next new date and get used to saying them without having to think. You want to be able to get your lies right even when you are exhausted and have had lots of drinks.

Try and keep your story simple. Lots of cheating guys try to include levels of detail in their explanations that they would never include in an answer to their wife when they were not cheating. If you are a guy who usually just mumbles a few things about what you have been doing, do not feel that you should embellish and colour up your stories on your cheating day.

Acting normal is the main thing. So, start by noticing how you answer your wife when things are absolutely fine, and she's just being nosey and practise copying those responses for when you are in trouble.

Never try and argue or fight when you are drunk. The worst thing is when some Dutch courage gives you the idea that you think you can fool her. So when you have been drinking a lot, do not bother getting into discussions with her.

Remember, do not repeat her question; a quick answer is the best answer. You should also practise how you will respond even if she is just a little suspicious. At the very least, you must prepare answers for the obvious questions like:

Where are/were you?
I rang your office. They said you left hours ago.
Susie saw you at lunch with someone. Who was that?
Why do you smell like fragrance?
Why do you smell like smoke?
Are you having an affair?
I know you are lying.

The approach you choose depends on how well you know your wife and what her response is likely to be.

Is your wife only interested because she feels she should care for the sake of her power position in the relationship or some philosophical stand for all women, when really, she would rather not ask, and not know?

Is she likely to be genuinely furious and want to divorce?

Is she gullible and likely to truly believe what you say?

Is this time likely to be "the straw that breaks the camel's back"?

Does she have evidence that you cannot deny?

In the last case (and only in that case), follow the advice in the chapter in this book on what to do when caught. In all other cases, it is just another speed bump in the road.

The lover is not your soul mate

Do not let your extramarital fling turn into the romance of your life.

In the George Clooney film *Up in the Air*, the hero thinks he is experiencing the romance of his life while his lover is just treating him as an affair. Clooney's character does not even know that she is married. Her mistake was not to end it once it got too serious. Instead, she ran the very real risk of having him interact with her family. Do not let this happen to you.

If you are worried that you are falling in love with her, do not try and tone it down, you are better off ending it. There are opportunities with other women that you can explore. It is important to remember that you went into this with a plan, to have some fun on the side. Stick to the plan. Not only will you become careless when you are in love, but we all know that when you are in that state, you make stupid decisions.

Don't be careless

Men get caught because they get lazy, drunk or very unlucky.

Most men who are caught out cheating are caught because they got careless and didn't follow the rules. It is as simple as that. There are bookshelves full of psychological texts about men trying to sabotage their relationships and deliberately trying to get caught — this does not apply in most cases. Let's be honest; you are a busy man with a marriage, probably a family, a job and a woman on the side. Sometimes it's all too much to cover your tracks. But failing to cover your tracks is what will get you caught, it's as simple as that. Check all the details - the little things.

Most importantly, when you are angry, tired or drunk, do not try and send emails or texts! You are a grown man - simply make it a hard and fast rule. If you cannot hold off, you will use the wrong phone or the wrong name. You will send a message with your office footer or text your wife a message you intended for your girlfriend. The list of potential tipsy text problems is awfully long.

Coincidences

From my Past: Katrina the Flight Attendant

Lesson - You may find unexpected coincidences

Stupid things can happen. I once took my mistress Katrina to a theatre show. It was one of those big nights out, everybody dressed up, but I found it tedious and a waste of money. Two days later, my wife gave me tickets to the same show for my birthday! Now not only did I have to pretend to be interested twice, but I had to seem shocked at all the right points. These sorts of crazy coincidences will happen. They are annoying, but a small price to pay for having the kind of fun that you can have sleeping around.

Katrina is an international flight attendant, and I met her on board. She assures me that the women working in first and business class on long-haul routes are not "hit upon" nearly as often as you might guess. Anyway, after a few hours of on-board chit chat (I had followed my usual cheater habit and given her only my middle name), I asked for her number. She later asked about my name – she had checked the flight manifest, and she knew who I was. We caught up in different cities over the next six months. I don't remember the reason for our disagreement now, but one day I broke things off with her, and we had one of those conversations where I pretended not to care. However, Kat was quite upset; she explained that she had to fly to Tahiti in the morning and would be happy to be away from me.

Later that evening, my widowed mother called me to explain that she was going on a vacation and would be flying to Tahiti in the morning. Oh no... there was only one flight between the two places tomorrow. So my recently scorned side-chick would be taking care of my mother! My name is reasonably unusual, and I know that Katrina checks passenger manifests. So after agonising for a while – I went to see my mom. I played it very cool but explained that someone pretty on the plane might make a scene tomorrow over a personal matter with me. My mother was so sanguine about it; she correctly assumed that "whatever I was trying not to talk about was *over*" and waved her finger, "Mark, it would have been better if you had mentioned something earlier, I would just have moved my flight". My mom has never mentioned it again, and certainly not to my wife.

XXI.

When you do get caught

"I did not have sexual relations with that woman."

-Bill Clinton

There are some key steps you must take, assuming you want to keep your marriage. To be brutally practical, even if you would rather be out, you do not want to be under pressure to have your marriage end immediately before you can make a good exit plan.

First, make sure you have really been caught.

When I was 18 years old, I took up skydiving. These were both static line drops and accelerated free-falls from 10,000 feet. There were numerous dams in the area where I used to jump, and new parachutists often used to land in the water. For some reason, parachutists are far more scared of drowning under a parachute that landed in the water than they are of jumping out of aircraft. A common problem was that parachutists would start to take off their chute by undoing the *Capewells* or 3-rings, when they thought they were going to land in the dam or lake. This would be fine — except when descending in a parachute, it is extremely hard to judge exactly how far you are above water. It is much easier to judge your height when you are above land and can see the height of trees, for example. So junior parachutists kept taking off their chute before they actually hit the water, then they would

XXI | When You Do Get Caught

fall freely without it from heights of up to one hundred feet, breaking ankles and legs. The training mantra at the parachute school soon became, "You are not in the water if your feet do not feel wet. You cannot take your parachute off until your feet are in the water".

It is well worth remembering this when accused of adultery. Make sure you are really caught before you start taking off your parachute and making admissions.

When I was in boarding school, I forged some paperwork to allow some friends to have a weekend away from the school. Because of rumours amongst the boys. I was suspected, but nobody could prove a thing. One night at 2 AM, a friend of mine was woken and was told that I had confessed, and he was asked why he had previously lied about it. He lost his nerve and apologised. If only he could have held the line. Of course, I would never confess.

This is the equivalent of when your wife says, "I honestly don't mind – I just want to know that I'm not crazy – I know most of it already". NO NO NO she does not. Hold your line.

If you feel you can get away with it, lie. Most of the world expects a married man to lie when confronted with suggestions of infidelity. Including your wife! Sometimes she will be relieved to hear that she is wrong (of course, you know she is spot-on.)

If you are really caught, here are the steps you may follow:

Step One: Apologise sincerely.

Say that you know you were so wrong. You have to say it didn't mean anything (it's cheesy, but it will save her some hurt).

Step Two: Explain it's already over, even if it isn't.

You know your wife, for some wives it can be best to say it

was only once, or if you think she is unlikely to believe that, twice. For example, it can sometimes be better to say you were with an online escort rather than somebody with whom you might fall in love.

Step Three: Ask for her forgiveness.

You truly do love her, and you know it was stupid. Please will she give you a chance to make it up to her?

Step Four: Suggest marriage counselling.

This is one that wives rarely expect; say that this may just be a way for you both to get past it. It is the best distraction from her immediate reaction of wanting to kick you out, and may just save your marriage.

Now, if you survive this first assault wave, you may have to give up some things, eat humble pie and generally be the perfect husband for a while. It's a very good idea to truly stop your affair. Some women have been known to engage detectives at this point. Your wife will be in super-spy mode, and you certainly don't need evidence of continuing, whether for legal or just for marriage reasons.

Marriage counselling is not there to make cheaters feel good. I do not know if there is such a thing as a friendly male marriage counsellor, but when I went, we saw a woman. She was horrible. It was clear that she saw it as her mission in life to have my wife divorce me. I only went a few times, long enough for my wife to decide she had also had enough of it and to feel she had done the right thing as a cheated wife.

XXII.

The Best Cheaters I Ever Met

As well as extensive research, the content in this book comes from my lifetime of skills and experience cheating as a married man. I have slept with dozens of different women, and some of my extramarital affairs spanned many years. But... as they say, whatever boat you buy, there is always a guy with a bigger boat. I have encountered a few star cheaters in my life. If cheating were an Olympic sport, these guys would be on the dais at the medal presentation. These are their stories:

The college Casanova

When I was nineteen, I shared an apartment with my fellow university student Lee. Every one of us knows a guy who magically always has a pretty woman with them - for me, that was Lee. The secret to Lee's success was that he simply did not mind rejection. He genuinely believed that there were so many fish in the sea that the girl he was talking to at the moment could either take him or leave, and if necessary, he could be very quickly on to the next one.

Like most young guys starting out in the world, I considered myself lucky if a girl even spoke to me. Lee was always lucky. He had a regular girlfriend who was super attractive, loving and besotted with him. Lee however, had embraced the freedom of college, having emerged from the limitations of boarding school, and he was going to live it up. Lee was one of those roommates who didn't bother to dampen down the shouts, sexy moans, screams and yells coming from his bedroom, just because he knew that I was at home. He certainly didn't worry that I might be embarrassed to hear him or at least upset that I was missing out.

One Saturday afternoon, I came back from playing football and heard the distinctive sounds of active, youthful sex in Lee's bedroom. I thought to myself about how lucky he was and went about making myself something to eat in the kitchen.

Shortly afterwards, the doorbell rang. As I was walking to answer the door, my roommate Lee poked his head out of his bedroom door and yelled, "Whatever you do, don't answer that door - that'll be my girlfriend; she is due here now". To this day, I don't know who was in his bedroom - whoever it was rapidly became aware that Lee had a girlfriend and that together they were cheating on her. Not that it posed a problem, the cries, moans, and shrieks coming from the room resumed shortly thereafter.

The last time I saw my old roommate was twenty years later. We had a late-night cocktail bar catch-up on what we had been doing, and there were lots of drinks. Then, in what must be a world record, Lee admitted to his infidelity on his recent honeymoon. He explained to me that he thought it was important not to get stuck in a rut. He had, at the time, been married for six days.

Lee reminds me of that old Swedish story about the man who propositioned every woman he ever met. Well... he got a lot of knock backs, but then again...

Takeaway message: You're already married - you don't need to worry about rejection, and that's why you can happily try as often as you want

XXII | The Best Cheaters I Ever Met

If the phone call is not for me – it must be for him

The next expert cheater who had an impact on me was Alejandro. I was 23 years old, in graduate school and sharing a house with him as my new roommate. We had met through mutual friends. This was about the time that mobile cell phones were just becoming popular, but neither Alejandro nor I had one. Instead, our shared house had an old-fashioned landline phone which we both used. I had been living there for three or four days when I heard the phone ring. I answered it and was speaking to a young woman asking to speak to Daniel. Disappointed that she didn't wish to speak to me, I responded, "Sorry, but there's no Daniel at this number".

Suddenly I saw my roommate hurtling towards me. He grabbed the phone from my hand without apology. Later, after the phone call, Alejandro explained that if anybody ever rang for any name I didn't know, and he was not at home, he would greatly appreciate it if I simply said that the person with whatever name was requested was out at the moment. I should then take a message for him. I asked what exactly he meant, and he explained his system of dating several different women at once, each one with a different name for him. Then, as one dropped off his list, he reused that name with the next and newest one.

Alejandro not only cheated, but he had a system; he made plans. For him, half the fun was seeing how many girls he could date simultaneously. He managed a roster just like a football team manager or ancient harem master.

Takeaway message:

Be creative - there are lots of ways to make this happen

Venice, Texas

The Danieli hotel in Venice, Italy is one of the world's best hotels. It has a spectacular view right across the Grand Canal to the islands. You can literally race one of the James Bond - Venice speedboat taxis up a canal and right inside the hotel. Even the new wing of the hotel is several hundred years old. I had wanted to stay at the Danieli for decades, and I was finally staying there with my wife.

Even in the winter low season, I was paying about $1200 per night for a mid-range room with that magical view. I was feeling rather good about myself until I went to check in. At the Danieli reception desk (an impressive welcome where the staff speak no fewer than five languages each), I was checking in beside a 60-year-old Texan, complete with his hat. Standing next to my Texan neighbour was an absolutely gorgeous mid 20s blonde, complete with an enhanced chest that would make any porn star proud. The Texan was clearly upset. As I wondered how anyone could be unhappy in this place, I listened in to his conversation at reception:

"I am not happy with my suite; I would like something nicer".
"Of course, sir, what is it that you are looking for?"
"Something much bigger."
The check-in clerk tapped away at his keyboard...
"Sir, we can give you one of our signature suites for the week."
"That sounds better."
"That will be €3400 per night Sir"
(that was over US$4000 each day!)
"Okay."

.... "plus, breakfast!"

XXII | The Best Cheaters I Ever Met

"Whatever, as long as it is sorted... oh by the way, from Saturday onward, I will need another room, near to mine, for my girlfriend here, my wife is arriving for the last two or three days."

"Of course, sir".

With everybody smiling, the receptionist went to show the Texan and his cheerleader girlfriend to his new suite.

Takeaway message:

Be bold - fortune favours the brave

Wife for a week

Rod was the simply most brazen cheater I ever met. This guy was unashamedly out and proud. I had just turned forty and Rod, who was sixty, was the CEO at a small company which was one of my clients. Meetings with him usually involved an exceedingly long lunch. The maître d' at every fashionable restaurant seemed to know Rod by name.

As I did every year, I travelled to a large national industry conference. I was amazed at the welcome drinks function when I noticed Rod was there with his arm around... his personal assistant. I thought I was brave, but surely this was pretty high risk. So imagine my amazement when I saw Rod's PA was wearing a badge with his real wife's full name. The two workmates and lovers were sharing a hotel room. There was absolutely no work reason for his assistant to be there. It was just one of those very male conferences where there is so much social and fun activity that men like to take their wives, who typically take part in a parallel social program. Rod's PA even went on all the social day tours badged as his wife, without him.

I've never seen anybody quite as blasé about their infidelity as Rod. Of the five hundred people at this conference, there must have been at least fifty guys who knew that she was not his wife, as well as many wives who had met his real wife the previous year. As much as Rod was shameless, his assistant seemed to enjoy playing the role of somebody else. To this day, I do not know which of them was having more fun with the cheating.

Takeaway message:

Yes, sometimes she enjoys the fact you are cheating as much as you do

XXIII.

Conclusion

So now we have taken a tour together through the landscape of affairs, mistresses and lovers. Since there are so many different ways that you can find sexual enjoyment outside of your marriage, if you decide to proceed with an affair, one of the methods in this book will almost certainly work for you. I wish you success, fun and happiness. You deserve it.

If you are interested in a range of additional guides to improving your enjoyment and fulfilment in life, I strongly recommend the Man You Want to Be series of books, Ebooks and audiobooks. They are all designed to help you have the kind of life you deserve. Leave your email on the website, and you will be first to know as new guides are released.

www.manyouwanttobe.com

www.Cheater.guide

XXIV.
Author Biography

Mark Fanon has lived in seven countries and worked in many more. He speaks several languages and has degrees in business from three universities. After spending many years learning how to enjoy lovers outside his home, without causing problems inside it, Mark is enjoying himself while keeping his marriage.

Following a C-Suite career in oil and gas corporations, Mark is now an Executive coach and frequent guest lecturer. Mark's books, audiobooks, and podcasts focus squarely on how to help men enjoy the lives their hard work should bring them.

www.MarkFanon.com

www.ingramcontent.com/pod-product-compliance
Lightning Source LLC
Chambersburg PA
CBHW072337300426
44109CB00042B/1662